AIRCRAFT MONOGRAPH

ROBERT MICHULEC

HEINKEL
He111

AJ•PRESS

AIRCRAFT MONOGRAPH 2

On cover: Heinkel 111 H–16 of 5./KG 27 on Eastern Front, 1943.

Paint:Jaroslaw Wróbel

COPYRIGHT © – Agencja A.J.–PRESS – 1994, POLAND
P. O. Box 73
80–461 GDAŃSK 45
tel. (0-58) 56-04-23, 56-34-76

English Edition Published for:
BOOKS INTERNATIONAL
69B Lynchford Road
Farnborough, Hampshire GU14EJ, England
Telephone: 0252 – 376564, Fax 0252 – 370181

Editor in Chief: **Adam Jarski**
Cover painting: **Jarosław Wróbel**
Colour Plates: **J. Wróbel, S. Zajączkowski, K. Cieślak**
Book Design: **Jarosław Wróbel, Adam Jarski**
Assistant Editor: **Barry Ketley**
Drawings: **Witold Hazuka, Archiwum**
English Edition edited by: **Barry Ketley** and **Robert Michulec**

Printed in Poland by: Drukarnia Oruńska,
Gdańsk, ul. Małomiejska 41, tel. (0-58) 39-41-22

ISBN 83–86208–12–0

I would like to thanks to:
the Crew of the Instituto de Historia y Cultura Aeronautica, the Crew of
the Museum of Aviation in Cracow, Bernád Denés and Knut Erik Hagen
for help in providing photos.
Author

BOOKS INTERNATIONAL TRADE REPRESENTATION IN EUROPE:

POLAND, CZECH REPUBLIC, SLOVAKIA, HUNGARY, RUSSIA AND EASTERN EUROPE:
BOOKS INTERNATIONAL
Ul. Lubelska 30/32
03 – 308 Warszawa
POLAND
Tel. & Fax (2) 619–60–57

AUSTRIA, SWITZERLAND, ITALY:
Mr. Juliusz Komarnicki & Mr. Patrick Bygate
Casella postale 196
CH–6900 Massagno
Switzerland
Tel.: 41-91-571539. Fax: 41-91-567865

BELGIUM, LUXEMBOURG, The NETHERLANDS
Mr. Reinier Pleysier
PO Box 166
8180 AD Heerde
Netherlands
Tel.: 31-5782-5203. Fax: 31 5782 5243

GERMANY
Mr. Robbert Pleysier
Walkottelanden 72
7542 MT Enschede
Netherlands
Tel.: 31-53775377. Fax: 31 53 778298

FRANCE, GREECE, YUGOSLAVIA
Mr. Graham Powell
11 Meadow Court Close
Bournemouth, Dorset BH9 2BT
England
Tel.: 0202 528263. Fax: 0202 537595

PORTUGAL, SPAIN, GIBRALTAR
Mr. Patrick Bygate
Casella postale 196
CH–6900 Massagno
Switzerland
Tel.: 41-91-571539. Fax: 41-91-567865

DENMARK, FINLAND, ICELAND, NORWAY, SWEDEN
Mr. Juliusz Komarnicki
Casella postale 196
CH–6900 Massagno
Switzerland
Tel.: 41-91-571539. Fax: 4191 567865
and
Mr. Ove Poulsen
PKB OBp International Marketing
Hegnet 13
DK–2600 Glostrup
Denmark
Tel.: 45-42-965060. Fax: 45-42-965060

A couple of the He 111P–1, the nearest of them coded 25+E33, of III/KG255 with experimental prewar camouflage.
(MAP)

THE LEGEND IS BORN

One of the many legends that make up the history of World War II is the story of the 'mail plane bombers' created by the German aircraft industry during the early stages of the development of the Luftwaffe. According to the story, the Germans built these bombers in the guise of civil aircraft and then almost overnight turned them into warplanes to terrify the innocent populations of Europe. This is not, of course, the literal reality, but in every legend there is some truth. It is a fact that the Germans created several fast designs in the 1930's, but only three were planned from the outset as a single aircraft for two essentially different roles. Since a fighter of the time was hardly suitable for carrying mail and passengers in peacetime, the only logical type that could do so would have to be a large, capacious airplane with at least two engines. In short, a 'passenger bomber'. Possibly as a result of the economic conditions of the 1930s this concept of quick civil-to-bomber conversions was not unique to Germany as the British, Dutch and Americans all developed bomber versions of what were originally civilian transport designs. However, the political and economic situation in Germany in 1933 – 35, shortly after Adolf Hitler became Chancellor of the Third Reich, was such that it was expedient not to boast too loudly of technological developments. Although Hitler's longer term aim was the creation of modern and powerful armed forces, German industry was not then capable of rapid development and full-scale production; moreover the announcement of such production plans would have warned other countries of his march towards rearmament and the breaking of the Versailles Treaty limitations. There were in addition cogent economic and military reasons for building a fast high speed airliner and a modern bomber based on the same airframe. At the time it was almost inevitable that the civil aircraft would be built in smaller numbers, with consequent higher unit costs if built alone, than if a short series of civil aircraft were built parallel with a bomber derivative. Only later was it found that the concept was

The He 111V3 was almost the same as the V1, and was a prototype aircraft for He 111A bomber.

flawed in that the civil versions were relatively expensive in operation, and for this reason the civil variant of the Heinkel He 111 was ultimately terminated [1]. The Germans were not alone in finding adaptations of one type to another less than satisfactory in the secondary role. The military version of the British Bristol 142 passenger aircraft, the *Blenheim*, and the American B–18 bomber based on the Douglas DC–3 both failed to live up to their original expectations. There was, however, another reason for pursuing the concept from the German point of view in that Lufthansa, the main potential customer for the civil He 111, would form the core of the Luftwaffe transport service in time of war. In this case it would be logical to have similar spares for both transport and bomber units [2].

The decision to build a dual civil/military aircraft was thus based upon several interacting reasons, the sum of which formed the basis for the first generation of bombers for the Third Reich, one of which, the He 111, served until the end of war. This publication presents the history of this famous, yet paradoxically little known design.

THE *FLYING SPADE*

On January 31, 1933, Hitler took complete control of Germany, and immediately began to accelerate the policies he had already started to set in place. His policies, especially in foreign affairs, were based upon boldness and risk, mer-

cilessly exploiting the weaknesses and mistakes of other European governments. Similar principles ruled the German armed forces. According to these unwritten rules the newly created German army regarded bomber aircraft as a principal defence element. This doctrine was based upon the Douhet theory, according to which an enemy could be defeated by an air force alone, provided it possessed a huge fleet of bombers capable of destroying the enemy's air forces, then his factories and the capital city. The Germans extracted from this theory what was of most value to them, namely that a single air raid of 500 bombers [3] against the capital of the country which would not accept the German will, or would dare to pose any threat to the Third Reich, would be decisive.

From today's viewpoint this doctrine seems very brutal, but it should not be forgotten that under the terms of the Treaty of Versailles Germany's army was heavily constrained, consequently the Germans felt the need for military power to regain their sovereignty in order to protect the sate from foreign dictate and to resist violations of the borders and the territory, as had happened in the Rheinland in 1923. The bomber force would protect the development of German industry and the army.

First studies of modern bomber development were carried out at the end of 1933, but not before spring of the following year did the RVM [4] decide that in spite of all the difficulties and

3

The He 111V5 coded D — APYS later reengined with DB 600A and recoded D — AJAK. The prototype aircraft for the He 111B bomber.

Above: An example of a late He 111B–1 of the early series. Note lack of cut-outs in the exhaust manifold cover, *Ikaria*, not installed fin and cross-bar in the middle of the water coolers. Also note missing bomb sight (but there is something in its place).

(MVT via M. Krzyżan)

Below: Another, very similar to previous one, example of the early He 111B–1. Note all standard details: cover of supercharged air inlet, exhaust pipes and their covers with cut-outs, surface oil coolers, fins at the lower engine cowling surfaces and cross-bar before water coolers.

(MVT via M. Krzyżan)

problems that work should start immediately. The most experienced companies, Heinkel Flugzeugwerke AG and Junkers Flugzeug und Motorenwerke AG were to develop aircraft capable of meeting the requirements of the coming era. The principal specifications called for 350 km/h speed, 1000 kg bomb load, 1000 km range, modern design and a crew of four. For many reasons as discussed earlier, a civil airline aircraft would also be developed from the same design, this variant being totally dependent upon the military project, the specifications only covering internal layout. The first RVM order called for 5 prototypes. Two of these, the second and fourth would be built for civil purposes, while the remaining three, bearing odd numbers, would be military variants. In the Heinkel company the 'civil bomber' project was entrusted to the Gfnter brothers, Siegfried and Walter, the designers of the Heinkel He 70, which can be described without exaggeration as the direct forerunner of the He 111 bomber. The bomber they designed featured the same shape of rear fuselage, the same tail planform and almost identical wings. Even though both designs differed in technological respects (the He 70 structure being mainly wood), the general concept and engineering solutions were extremely similar.

Preliminary calculations and design work was carried out in a very short time so that the first flight of the He 111 took place on February 24, 1935. In the absence of the Heinkel chief test pilot, Jucke, the first flight was completed at Marienehe by Gerhard Nitschke. The maiden flight proved the excellent flying and handling characteristics of the aircraft. Later tests also showed that the design suffered very few teething troubles, thus confirming the success of the designers. The first bomber prototype, called He 111a, was powered by inline BMW VI 6,0Z engines rated at 600 hp (490 kw), with an empty weight of 5,782 kg and an AUW of 7,590 kg and reached a top speed of 348 km/h. Fuel tankage allowed for a range of some 1,500 km and maximum ceiling approached 6,600 m. Shortly after the first, two more prototypes appeared at the airfield, but because of pressure from the authorities and the priority given to the bomber version, it was the third prototype, the He 111c, that flew next, on March 12, while the He 111b was not flown for the first time until April 9. As a result the designations were changed, the combat variant becoming the He 111b and the civil one the He 111c. The tests at Rechlin and Staaken went on smoothly and upon their completion the RLM ordered production of the A–0 series based on the He 111b. Upon returning the aircraft to the works several modifications were introduced and further testing was carried out on all three prototypes, disclosing information on shortcomings in the design, and, above all, data concerning the best wing airfoil. Since the designers could not reach a conclusion as to the best wing airfoil and planform of the future bomber, it was decided that each of the three prototypes would have a slightly different wing. All information gathered during the tests would then be used in the He 111d and He 111e built in the second half of 1935. Before the two prototypes were rolled out however, the designation system was changed from the old letter based system to a new alphanumeric one, consequently the aircraft were renamed, the He 111d becoming the He 111V4 and the He 111e the He 111V5.

Previous designation	New designation	Civil registration	Name
He 111a	He 111 V1		
He 111c	He 111V2	D–ALIX	'Rostock'
He 111b	He 111V3	D–ALES	
He 111d	He 111 V4	D–AHAO	'Dresden'
He 111e	He 111V5	D–APYS	

The He 111V4 was first flown in late 1935 and on January 10 of the next year was shown to the foreign press, while the third military prototype, the He 111V5 was first flown in early winter 1936. (Needless to say, this version was not shown to any outside witnesses). This aircraft was originally fitted with BMW VI 6,0Z engines, which despite a shorter wing and other small modifications, only increased its speed by 11 km/h. Following closely after the disastrous test results of the He 111A–02 and 03 from the six-aircraft pre-production series which had been carried out at Rechlin in the early spring of 1936, led to a mixed response from the RLM decision-makers. Based on the V3, but completely redesigned to meet the military requirements, the machines were 519 kg heavier than the original, whilst installing gun positions and making the glazed nose longer by 1,2 m effected the clean aerodynamics of the fuselage and the top speed fell to 308 km/h. Lack of engine power was evident, this leading to additional problems with low speed handling (during take-off and landing the aircraft completely lost its previous excellent characteristics). Because of these shortcomings production of the He 111A series was halted immediately, and the very existence of the He 111 was in danger for a short period.

To solve the problem it was decided to replace the engines with new DB 600A–0 types, theoretically rated at 1000 hp (740 kw), but which, however, did not yet develop full power. This led in turn to new problems. The new engines were fitted with the old cooling system, completely unsuitable for the much more powerful DB 600. The designers soon solved that by enlarging the oil coolers which in turn led to replacing the standard oil cooler with a surface type and repositioning it under the wing on both sides of the engine. So modified the He 111V5 was re-registered as D–AJAK (previously D–APYS), was accepted by he RLM and became the template for a production bomber.

The favourable opinion of the He 111V5 which came from Rechlin in the winter of 1936, staing that the V5 represented a substantial improvement compared to the A–0, caused the decision to re-start production of the Heinkel bomber. Accordingly, production of the first pre-series batch of He 111B–0 was started at Marienehe in the autumn of that year. This differed from the prototype (He 111 V5) by being fitted with production DB 600A engines rated at 1000 hp (740kW) and full combat equipment. One of the first aircraft assembled was passed as well as in the case of the V5. In spite of the satisfaction with the new variant, a list of short-comings and failures was sent to the factory for modifications to the production model. The final verdict was, however, evidently favourable for the Ernst Heinkel company; the He 111 was 'fit for military service'.

After the production lines were readied, in November 1936, mass production of the first true production variant of the bomber, the He 111 B–1, commenced. Most likely early examples of the first series of the B–1 were all fitted with the same engines as the B–0, but these were subsequently replaced with simpler and less powerful DB 600C types, rated at 880 hp (650 kW). Many modifications were applied on the production lines (which produced 20–25 air-

The He 111A–0 bomber with a new nose section, propellers and spinners.

craft a month). These ranged from minor, such as replacing the aerial mast with a streamlined version and then repositioning it to port so that it would not interfere with the pilot's opening hatch, or slight changes to the shape of the exhaust manifold; to major changes such as repositioning the oil cooler from beneath the wing to under the liquid cooler mounted under the engine. Moreover, the B–1 differed from the B–0 in having an increased combat weight of 9300 kg, and the middle B–1 series were fitted with new 'Ikaria' forward gunner nacelle (these had been thoroughly tested on the He 111 V3). Basic combat equipment of the aircraft included three 7,9mm MG 15 machine guns placed in forward, dorsal and ventral positions, an FuG III radio set and a Gv 219d bombsight which allowed fairly precise dropping of the 1500 kg of bombs carried in the vertical bomb bays in the central fuselage. The He 111 could carry even 2000 kg bombs but due engines' lack of power this model had bomb load only 1500 kg for 1600 km range or 2000 kg for 900–1000 km flight. This second solution was puted into combat practice very rarely, because such short range was not enoughed to penetrating enemies territory. The B–1 was manufactured until June 1937 when all factories switched to the B–2 model, already being built from May 4 at Oranienburg. The He 111 B–2 was fitted with newer, more powerful DB 600 CG engines rated 950 hp (750 kW), which allowed for increased capabilities. Another modification, probably introduced in the summer of 1937, was the use of a new type of engine cowling, necessitated by the troublesome exhaust manifolds. In place of six separate exhaust outlets, partially covered with a streamlined fairing, a single exhaust duct was introduced which carried the exhaust gases under the wing. Just as it was in the earlier variant, the manifold was covered with a fairing which, also similarly to the earlier variant, was usually removed by the ground crew in the units. The difference between this fairing and the old

one used in the B–1, was that the later type was shaped to exactly fit the exhaust pipe which was covered completely. The same solution was introduced on the B–1s used in Spain, but the engine cowling not being adapted for this element necessitated positioning of the exhaust pipe at a greater angle, this leading to less effective expulsion of the exhaust gases which led in turn to a further drop in speed. Another difference which distinguished the B–2 from the B–1 models was the re-shaped engine cowling just above the exhaust manifold which lacked a carburettor air intake fairing. This could be found on the B–1 as well, provided that the aircraft was so fitted at the factory, since this portion of the engine cowl was fixed to the engine bed. Thanks to all these modifications, and to the new engines, top speed of the B–2 rose from 369 km/h to some 385 km/h with AUW reaching 10,000 kg. This included 1500 kg of bombs and standard combat equipment with enough fuel tankage to carry the 10 tonnes across 1660 km. Such specifications eventually satisfied everyone, and the aircraft was accepted by the Luftwaffe as its best and basic bomber.

After autumn 1937 information about the 'Berta' is scarce. This does not mean, however, that the variant's history ended, since according to all available data, manufacture of this version, albeit with modifications, continued until summer 1938 and totalled a large number of aircraft. It is known that on September 19, 1938 Luftwaffe units had 272 He 111B, 61 more aircraft were sent to Spain, some 10% were lost in accidents and not less than 50 were delivered to training units. This gives a total of about 450 aircraft. However, according to the sequence of He 111B werk nummers it is possible that not less than 550 aircraft were manufactured.This number comes from comparision of known serials, W.Nr. 1003 [5] on one of the first B–1s and W.Nr. 1517 on a B–2 of KG26 [6]. Additional information is provided by two photographs showing two very different B–2s carrying num-

Below: One of the middle series He 111B–1 planes, D–AANV, with surface oil coolers and „Ikaria" turret. Aircraft painted in standard RLM 62, 63, 64 and 65 colours camouflage, with white spinners and silver propeller blades.

(MVT via M. Krzyżan)

Two photos of almost the same aircraft. Above the He 111 J–1 executive version (W.Nr. 554), and below, late He 111B–2 with DB 600G engines (W.Nr. 552).

bers 552 and 554 (or W.Nrs. 1552 and 1554). These He 111B–2 of the last production series differed only in engines. Instead of the DB 600CG they used the DB 600G featuring new exhaust manifolds and a longer carburettor air intake. The first stage of of He 111 development testing was carried out between 1936 and 1938, using three basic prototypes, the He 111V6, V7 and V8, based on the He 111B–0. This was planned to include several tests to establish development in three principal directions: new

power plants; a new wing, easier to manufacture; and a new cockpit arrangement. For the first of these, the He 111 V6 (D–AXOH) was allocated. It was originally powered by Junkers Jumo 210 Ga engines, but these proved underpowered and during the summer of 1937 they were replaced with the then latest model, Jumo 211A rated at 1000 hp (740 kW). Since these engines were heavier and their mountings not quite correct, they were handed back to Junkers, together with the aircraft, where the engine/main–plane

and engine/airscrew connections were tested thoroughly. The new VS–5 propellers were also tested at Junkers, but these failed in testing and in the subsequent He 111 models later variants of the VDM propeller were used. Introducing Jumo engines was only a question of time, however, since these were more convenient, less sophisticated and more reliable (for example they lacked the fuel injection system necessary in the fighter power plants, the Jumo 210 and DB 601), although they were a little heavier than the DB 601. It is worth noting that this aircraft, perhaps because of the long time it spent outside the Heinkel works, was still fitted with the original type forward gun position, like that of the He 111A. An additional modification on the V6 was the new pitot tube, repositioned from the navigator's position to the port wing. The second prototype, the V7 (D–AUKY), was used for testing new wing designs, which were to be less expensive, simpler and easier to manufacture. The final version was completely different to that used on all He 111 versions beginning from the V1. The mainplane was almost totally redesigned, especially ailerons and flaps, as well as fuel tanks and the whole wing leading edge. The purpose of the next prototype, the V8 (D–AQUO), initially used for various other tests, was to find the optimum shape for the cockpit, which was to be rebuilt to the new Luftwaffe standard. This demanded that from 1937 on, any new bomber was to feature a fuselage in which all, or most of the crew members, would be placed in a common area, covered by a single large glazed surface. Such a cockpit was supposed to enhance co-operation of the crew members and allow mutual help when needed. To respond to this principle all the bombers then at various stages of development, i.e. the Dornier Do 17, Junkers Ju 86, Junkers Ju 88 and the He 111, were redesigned. The latter differed from all the others in that its cockpit was streamlined into the fuselage outline. The whole front portion of the fuselage was redesigned and shaped between the nose and rear of the pilot station in the form of an inflated cigar. This produced a large space in which three crew members could easily work together in the completely glazed cockpit. Arrangement and equipment within the cockpit was not easy to finalise and it took much testing and experimentation before the final V8 version took to the air in January 1938.

The favourable conditions of the summer of 1937 allowed construction at Marienehe of subsequent prototypes which were to lead to the successor to the He 111B. The He 111 V9 (D–AQOX) was fitted with more powerful DB 600Ga engines rated at 1050 hp (770 kw) [these could in fact be of the DB 600G variant], basically differing from the earlier CG version in nothing but power rating and weight, increased by 10 kg, so the tests were a formality only. Switching production from 'Berta' to 'Dora' (He 111 D–1) was trouble free as the lack of structural changes led to no change in the production line tooling. The only differences between He 111D and He 111B were in modified or changed internal systems, and the only visible modification was the oval spinner taken from the Jumo 211 engines, covering the VDM propeller. The spinner also identified the electric starter that replaced the previous mechanical type. Thanks to all these slight modifications, the He 111D was destined to be series — produced as the successor to the 'Berta', even before testing the V9 began. In the early autumn of 1937 a short series of pre-production He 111D–0 left the Wismar factory, followed immediately by the first a few production machines. The new engines made this version superior to its predecessor as it was capable of reaching a top speed of 410 km/h, which allowed it to escape the fighters of some neighbouring countries, e.g. the Avia B-534, PZL P. 11, Fokker D-XVIII, Dewoitine D.501 or Polikarpov I–15 bis. Ironically, however, at the same time the results of tests with the Jumo 211A engined He 111V6 became known. The potential

Above: The He 111D–0 was not produced due realisation He 111E program. At this photo one of a few, coded D–AOHA.

(MAP)

Below: The He 111V23 with a new ventral pod.

of these engines which had been fitted by Junkers
was such that the decision was taken to abandon
the He 111 fitted with obsolete DB 600 engines
in favour of the new Jumo 211. Consequently,
production of the 'Dora' was halted at the very
beginning and soon cancelled. The few aircraft
completed (about 10 – 15, only three registrations are known – D–AYFO [He 111D–0],
D–AOKE and D–AOHA [both probably D–0
too]), were later used for test purposes.

At about the same time, one of the production aircraft, the B–0, designated V10 (D–
ALEQ) [6bis], was used for a series of important
tests in order to determine if, and where, to
position the oil cooler from under the liquid
cooler. Based on experience with the Jumo 211
powered He 111 V6 the company decided to
place the cooler above the engine and modify the
whole cooling system, making it similar to that of
the V6. Probably at the same time it was already
planned to interchange use of the Jumo 211 and
DB 601 engines. After successful tests this arrangement was used on the He 111G–4 (DB 600G
powered V16), the He 111G–5 for Turkey (DB
600Ga?), the He 111G–5 (DB 601A) prepared
for General Milch and the P variant which
entered service less than a year later.

In July 1937 another prototype, the V11 (D–
ARCG), with new innovations, developed from
one of the B–1s was flown. The aircraft was to
have been powered by Jumo 211A–3 engines [7],
but eventually the original DB 600CGs were
replaced with DB 600G types featuring new carburettor air intakes and exhaust manifolds. Its
role is not clear, but it was probably used to test
the latest modifications to these powerplants.
The test results were so attractive that the
decision was taken to introduce the modifications in production aircraft, without changing
the designation. Such aircraft were manufactured during the final period of He 111B–2 production and was a result of the He 111D cancellation.

At that time, in early 1937, RLM officials,
under pressure from the Turks who wanted the
latest He 111 version, and with utilisation of the
new tapered-wing factory in view, allowed the
creation of a new intermediate version of the
'one-eleven', by matching the previous He 111
with the new wing. After protracted negotiations
Turkey purchased 24 He 111D with new wings
and old engines (probably DB 600CG), designated in the meantime He 111F–1 by the RLM.
The order was followed by another for 5 He
111G–5, also with new wings, but with newer DB
600Ga engines.

The most important innovation in the
Turkish contract was the fuel tank fitted in the
port bomb bay which allowed this version of the
Heinkel to carry only 1000 kg, but across a
greater distance than a standard Luftwaffe He
111. The whole series was produced between
October and November 1937 – the first production F–1 being completed on October 19.

Cancelling the He 111D and offering this
version for export made the Heinkel works concentrate on the Jumo-powered 'Berta' successor,
designated He 111E, the ultimate version of
which was first flown in the winter of 1937. Upon
acceptance by the RLM, the He 111 V6 [8], with
a new radio system and other minor modifications, became a prototype of the 'Emil', production of which started in January 1938. Two pre-
series E–0s were followed by the short series of
20 – 40 E–1s. Needless to say, the more powerful
and reliable engines gave this first 'Emil' series
as high a combat capability as that of the 'Dora'.
In February 1938 the E–1 variant was replaced

**The He 111V19 (D–AUKY), the prototype of
the H bomber version.**

Above: A very rare version of the He 111 plane – the He 111J–1 version – photographed somewhere
in Germany, 1942.
(R. Michulec coll.)
Below: The He 111V8 with a new nose section. The old DB 600C engines and the lack of the ventral
pod are clearly visible. This experimental airplne was built on the basis of He 111B–1.

The He 111C–0 'Leipzig' at the civil airport waiting for passengers, 1937.

(MVT via M. Krzyżan)

by the generally similar E–3, while it was the E–4 and E–5 that introduced the first important modifications in offensive weapons resulting experience in the Spanish Civil War and with the F–1 for Turkey. The Luftwaffe command requested that the bombers be modified to allow carriage of larger bombs, able to destroy larger targets. In the case of the He 111, this was a much more serious problem than in other bombers, since it had two separate smaller bomb bays on both sides of the fuselage, rather than a single large one. The bombs, typically, for example, of 100 kg size, were attached vertically (fuse up) in four separate compartments which were too small to accept bomb sizes larger than 250 kg. This led to the E–4 version featuring a single external attachment for heavy bombs, fitted in the position occupied in previous variants by the bomb bay doors. The E–5 sub-variant was equipped with a similar attachment, and also with additional tanks for 835 litres of fuel and 115 litres of oil, fitted in place of one of the standard bomb bays. The external attachment system was later widely used both as standard

and in various combinations with internal bomb bays, which enabled Heinkel bombers to carry out various tasks, whether requiring long range or those where large or small size loads were involved. The E series aircraft had the highest AUW of all the early versions, the first to pass the 10,000 kg threshold. With the E–5 version it exceeded 11,000 kg. In this version the aircraft was capable of reaching a target 2200 km distant, but its speed was not exceeding 400 km/h. Equipment was also changed, e.g. the old bomb sight was replaced with the Lofte 7, used until the end of the war, and the forward MG 15 gun was replaced in the later series by an MG 17. From all series except the E–1, the Fubl 1 blind landing aid was installed, easily recognisable by horizontal aerials under the rear fuselage, while very early of that year (1938), modified vertical tail surfaces were introduced, with mass balanced rudder. Similar rudder balancing was simultaneously introduced on late B–2 (with DB 600 G engines) and J variants.

In parallel with the RLM 'Emil' contract, the Luftwaffe placed an additional order in spring

1938 for He 111E's with external stores, (including one similar to the Turkish F–1, with additional tankage), soon followed by an order for similar aircraft but with the new wing. While the E models, (E–4 and E–5), were bombers with a single external pylon, the new variant, called He 111F–4, was to have two pylons able to carry two heavy bombs and was powered by Jumo 211 A–1 engines. The RLM ordered 40 of these machines which were delivered in parallel with the early 'Emil' series in the winter of 1938. To conclude the description of this He 111 model it has to be said that the F–4 is something of a very rare variant and there is known only one photo of it. During the war, many of the best preserved E and F types were taken from air training schools and handed over to transport units, where some of them were modified in 1942 by the fitting of ETC pylons under the wings, between fuselage and engine nacelles. These enabled the carrying of larger, 700 kg supply pods, which could carry oversize loads.

Because the new models of the He 111 and Junkers Ju 88 were not appearing, and the Luftwaffe consequently lacked a good torpedo-carrying aircraft, at the end of 1937 the RLM contracted Heinkel to manufacture an additional series of 90 aircraft modified to carry torpedoes. The choice of Heinkel followed from the favourable experience of use of the He 111E–4 fitted with underfuselage overload hardpoints, and also from the free workforce at the Heinkel factories. The fact that the He 111 was at that time the best German bomber was also a contributory factor. Using the arrangements from the the E–4, E–5 and F–4, new attachments which could carry two 765 kg LT 5b aircraft torpedoes or two sea mines were fitted in place of the standard

bomb racks. All the specifications from both Luftwaffe and Kriegsmarine were collected and two prototypes were built: the V17 (D – ACBH) used as the prototype, and the V18 (D – ADUM), which served for evaluation of torpedo attachment possibilities and conditions [9]. After testing at Rechlin, Eckernforde and Leba (now Łeba, Poland), production started at the end of winter 1938. As in most of the previous versions the He 111J was powered with DB 600 Ga [10] engines, enclosed by partly modified cowlings (carburettor air intake) and fitted with new exhaust manifolds. This new version differed from late B–2 versions in more powerful engines (Ga instead of G), radio systems and the new wing.

According to the contract the aircraft was to carry two underfuselage adaptors. However, since the Kriegsmarine cancelled the land-based torpedo carrier programme, only the He 111J–0 series was built to this standard. The main part of the contract was delivered as standard bombers with internal bomb bays and delivered to ordinary bomber units. In total, 90 aircraft were built, none of which ever saw service with naval aviation units. All the Js were sent to bomber regiments, only to be phased out in 1939, and handed over to air training schools. The last aircraft were delivered to second-line units and were transferred in October 1939 to KGr 808.

The J type ended early Heinkel 111 development. As early as the turn of 1938, Heinkel A.G. started mass production of a new generation of the bomber that crowned its evolution and brought the original concept of the Günter brothers to its peak.

Until that time the Norddeutschen Dornierwerke, Arado Brandenburg/Havel, ATG at Leipzig and the main Heinkel works at Marienehe and Oranienburg, manufactured a total of 970 He 111s, both civil and military, in the following versions: 5 original prototypes; 6 He 111A; 550 He 111B; 6 He 111C; 10 He 111D; 220 He 111E; 64 He 111F; 10 He 111G/L and 90 He 111J. 130 of these were delivered to foreign customers.

Finally, the 'ghost' He 111 version, the He 111K, is worth mentioning here. This designa-

One of the early He 111P–1s at the factory airfield during engine test. Note standard exhaust manifold.

(MVT via M. Krzyżan)

tion appeared in 1937, when the world had already got to know about the He 111 from the official announcement of the civil variant and from the Spanish Civil War news. The Third Reich authorities confirmed the existance of the combat version, and named it officially as the He 111K (K standing for Kampfflugzeug — combat in German, but it means bomber aircraft). Thus there was something to use as a threat, while marking it difficult for foreign military intelligence to identify the aircraft.

The He 111 in civil guise

The civil He 111 versions were not used widely and were not even produced in small numbers. The reason is somewhat similar to that of the Junkers Ju 86 becoming a useful airliner. The Ju 86 was not a good bomber, while the He 111 was regarded as the best Luftwaffe medium bomber. Together with the prototypes, only 8 civil machines were built, of which three (V2, V4, and C–03) were handed over to the secret reconnaissance unit 'Kommando Rowehl' in 1937. A further 4 civil aircraft were built at the turn of 1937, including two powered by BMW 132 radial engines. All the G (in-line engines) and L (radial engines), [unofficial Lufthansa designations for Heinkel's G–3], aircraft had one thing in common — the new wing with the straight leading edge. The G–5, powered by the DB 600Ga (or DB 601A), of which 6 were built, was the last non-combat He 111 model. One of these, powered by DB 601's, was built as General Milch's personal aircraft, while the rest were built for Turkey where they served in a similar role to that of Milch's. The five Turkish He 111G–5s had the same wings as the He 111F–1.

A maid of all work

After long testing, the Günter brothers started work in 1938 on a completely new machine. The flight testing of two prototypes, the V7 (new wing) and V8 (new cockpit) were carefully watched, and the data gathered was quite promising. The wings had already been tested sufficiently, both in research and in operational use, and were already in production; the cockpit however posed many questions. In previous versions of the bomber the pilot's seat was raised a little and the controls arranged in a conventional way, but the requirement to concentrate all the flight navigational stations in one place posed some problems. To better use the room and to maximise the space available, it was shaped asymmetrically, with the starboard side straight and the port, pilot's section more rounded. Pilot, the crew commander, was seated on the port side; to his right the navigator worked using a folding seat which could be extended into a small

A photo of the aerial torpedo LT 5, in the background is a He 111H–4 or H–5. *(R. Michulec coll.)*

'bed' enabling him to both handle the forward gun and to work on the navigation in a 'lazy' position if desired. Thanks to the placement of the instrument panel above the pilot's head, the forward and downward field of view were excellent, which was useful during landing. Some problems were encountered during taxying, but this was solved by the use of an hydraulic jack which raised or lowered the pilot's seat. To prevent the pilot from injuring his head during this operation a back sliding cover of a slightly bulbous form was installed above him. A similar, partly glazed door was also fitted on the starboard side of the cockpit and was similarly used by the navigator. However, in this case the hatch was mainly important because in earlier navigator did not have a separate escape which could be dangerous in emergency situations.

There is not known a direct prototype prototype of the He 111P, but it is believed that it is the He 111 V7. However it isn't true, because the V7 was an experimental aircraft and not a prototype of production airplane version. The

aircraft featured the new wing, with a span of 22.50m (rather than the 22.61m of the earlier wing, but with the wing area identical at 86.50 sq. m). Other changes included a new redesigned cockpit (changed even compared to the He 111 V8), a new ventral gunner's position (from the V23), which enabled him to operate the gun in a prone position, new 1140 x 410 mm wheels, and many changed or modified internal systems. It was powered by two DB 601A engines, rated at 1100 hp (810 kw), but the engine installation was so designed that replacement with Jumo 211 engines posed no problems, so that the He 111 in the field, in emergency situations, could have two different engines fitted (DB and Jumo). The prototype first flew in the winter of 1938, series production commencing in late autumn of that year, which indicates the level of problems encountered during testing. First production He 111P–1s were delivered to units at the very end of 1938, raising much interest and controversy. Opponents were particularly suspicious of the cockpit layout, but the excellent performance

A very well known photo of the He 111H–2 plane of the ObdL reconnaissance unit, 1939. Note a overpainted letters and small cross at the lower wing surface and at the fuselage.

(MVT via M. Krzyżan)

Above: The early He 111H–6 with 'Ikaria' and a fix for additional MG 15 over it. Note a two different bomb racks under the fuselage (PVC 1006 and ETC 2000).

Below: One of not many, the He 111H–8 after force landing in England, spring 1941.

balanced all the shortcomings. The new Heinkel reached a top speed of 410 km/h at an altitude of 5000 m, so thanks to the new engines the service ceiling was increased by 1000 m while retaining the top speed. AUW rose to 12.200 kg, mainly because of a greater quantity of fuel which increased the range to 2100 km. and additional equipment. Excellent flying characteristics remained practically unchanged, as was defensive armament. In spite of suggestions from Spanish Civil War veterans, only three MG 15

7.9mm guns were left in the three gunners positions. Feeding from 75 round ammunition drums was their main shortcoming. Even though it only took seconds to change the drum, this could be fatal in combat (it only took a fighter some 3 seconds to fire a deadly burst). The feeding system was gradually changed, but it was not until the end of 1940 variant that all guns were fitted with ammunition belt containers to accommodate 500 or 1000 rounds per gun.

Two photos of the gliding torpedo LT 10 on the standard bomb rack of the He 111H–6.

(MVT via M. Krzyżan)

In its time the He 111P–1 counted among the worldRs leading bombers. Its British rival, the Vickers *Wellington* Mk I had essentially the same specifications, and could be regarded as equal. In the Soviet Union the Ilyushin DB–3 was the Heinkel's direct counterpart, but because of its special role it had twice the range but only half the bomb load and AUW. Neither France nor the USA had a bomber at that time which could compare with the German 'spade', but neighbouring Poland possessed an aircraft which even exceeded its German counterpart. The PZL P.37 Łoś' ('Elk') speed and range were nearly equal, while the bomb load was slightly greater than that of the He 111. Its main shortcoming compared to the Heinkel was inferior service ceiling and low resistance to damage. In parallel with the P–1, the H–1 version of the Heinkel was in production from the beginning of 1939. The H prototype, the V19 (D – AUKY) was built at the turn of 1938, based on a P–0, right after He 111P production commenced. The sole difference was in the Jumo 211 A–1 engines.

The P–1 was in production until May 1939 when the P–2, featuring a new FuG X radio set, started to leave the Marienehe and Wismar factories, while at Oranienburg and Brandenburg/Havel the He 111H–2 (since April 1939) and the P–2 were assembled. The H–2 also had the FuG X (S 10K and L transmitters and E 10K and L receivers) instead of the FuG III radio set (S 3a transmitter, E 2a and DLH E 20 receivers), and the Peil EP 1a radio finder (with a circular aerial) was replaced by the Peil G5, the latter in fact already fitted in the later H–1 series. The H–2 also differed from the H–1 in having more powerful Jumo 211 A–3 engines, rated at 1100 hp (810 kw), which had larger and more efficient oil coolers, and allowed few extra km/h.

Production was developing fast, and the He 111H became the main production model, though the P version, not wanted so much was also produced until mid-1940. This was caused by two interacting facts. First, because of the shortage of both engine types it was safer to build two bomber versions to avoid production holdups; second, the war was approaching and the Luftwaffe did not wish to enter it with old versions of the 'flying spade'.

The P–3 was another He 111 sub-variant, intended for pilot training, and differing from the combat aircraft in a rearranged cockpit. Instead of the navigator's folding seat, another more comfortable one was fitted for the instructor pilot, who also had a separate set of controls to allow him to correct pupil's errors. These aircraft had all the defensive and offensive armament removed, as well as any combat equipment.

The new He 111P and H were introduced into Luftwaffe service in autumn and winter of 1939 – 40, and offered improved combat capabilities and survivability when encountering enemy fighters, as well as modified internal systems. The necessity to improve the armament was testified to by the air combats over Poland which confirmed the earlier views of the Spanish

Civil War veterans. Since at the beginning of the war only machine guns were considered as standard bomber defence, the only way of increasing the 'spade's' defensive capability was by adding guns and gunnery positions. The H–3 and P–4 variants which appeared at the beginning of October 1939 and early 1940 respectively, each had three additional guns fitted. Each had a new gun position in the rear fuselage between the dorsal and ventral gunners. The new, fifth crew member manned, depending on the situation, two guns, in both rear fuselage windows. His position was not very comfortable (he was almost directly above the ventral gunner) and in practice he could only deter enemy fighters with additional fire. The third gun was installed in the front of the ventral cupola. This MG 15 was an additional gun to cover a previously blind area, and, just like the side guns, was to be manned by a single man with another task, the radio operator. His situation was not to be envied. He had to lie on his belly with his parachute on his back, and often his life jacket too, operate the rear ventral gun, and when needed, immediately change his position by 180o, aim and fire. In theory it was possible; in practice, impossible. This gun soon proved to be ineffective, so it was replaced with a cannon, or simply removed. Both designers and flying personnel gradually learned that in order to improve fire power, it was the calibre of the gun that had to be increased. Armour for both pilot and each of the rear gunners was an important innovation in the two almost identical series. The future was to prove however, that this was too small, too few and too thin. The He 111P–4 was additionally modified to a more versatile standard which involved fitting extra racks for large bombs. The novelty of this application was that instead of one older ETC pylon, two PVC 1006L were installed, thus covering both internal bomb bays, and that (like in the E–5) an additional internal fuel tank was fitted in the port bomb bay.

The H–4 underwent an identical modification. It was also fitted with two underfuselage racks for large bombs and the fuselage tank for 835 litres of fuel in one of the bomb bays which allowed the range to increase from 2060 km to 2600 km. The possibility of carrying 300, 600 or 900 litre tanks on external racks, which greatly extended the range was an additional advantage of the '4' model (and those with external pylons that followed).

The results of He 111H–4 development and use were so promising that both RLM representatives and Heinkel designers decided to go further and make the 'one-eleven' a long range bomber intended to carry the heaviest bombs.

Two photos of another special models of the He 111; a He 111H–15 (above) with 3 BV 246 flying bombs and (below) a H–12 with another Bv 143 flying bomb.

The resultant He 111H–5 was fitted with the new Jumo 211 F–1 engines [11], rated at 1300 hp (960 kw) that could be fed with either A2 or B4 grade fuel, two internal additional fuel tanks for 1670 litres and a little new underfuselage bomb carriage system. The main advantage of the new idea was the possibility of carrying a variety of bomb types, thanks to extra bomb rack 'fingers' installed between two standard PVC pylons in the bomb door. These were reinforced with special plates which allowed easy repositioning to fit different bomb sizes and shapes. Thanks to these the He 111H–5 could accept the then largest German bomb, the 2.5 tonne 'Max' (which could only be carried by the H–5). In theory, with 500 kg overload, the aircraft could carry the bomb over 1500 km, but in reality, in order to take off, the amount of fuel was limited to only 2060 litres in the main tanks, which only allowed about 1000 km range. On the other hand, the maximum range of this variant, with minimum bomb load (no more than 500 kg) rose to 3200 km! With

such a load the maximum take-off weight rose to almost 14.5 tonnes which was all that could be demanded of the He 111. The main shortcoming of the He 111H–5 was its take-off run, much bigger that of the fully laden H–4. An aircraft carrying maximum bomb load and with full fuel tanks could not clear the ground without a long concrete runway, and steering it in the air when it carried a 'Max' required high pilot skills.

At the time when the H series bloomed, the P was gradually fading away. Its latest modification, the He 111P–6 was powered with DB 601 N engines, rated at 1175 hp (865 kw), created for fighters and adopted to use the MW 50 mixture, so their value for bombers was rather limited, mainly because of the short service life and sensitivity. The limited value of these powerplants was quite obvious and, after a short series was manufactured in the summer of 1940, the Luftwaffe eventually abandoned this variant, thus bringing to an end the Daimler Benz – powered He 111 family.

A very nice photo of a He 111H–16 in flight over the Russian Front.

(MVT via M. Krzyżan)

The He 111H–18 equipped with the FuG 200 radar.

Before a new version arrived, some aircraft already in service were modified to carry out specialised night bombing missions. The first of these were He 111H–1x, H–2x and H–3x, fitted with the X–Geräte; the other being the He111H–5y [12] with Y–Geräte. Both systems were quite similar and came from the same source, the EBL 2 device used for landing under heavy weather. The system, slightly modified and named 'Knickebein', was adapted at the turn of 1939 to guide bombers at distances up to 500 km in the dark of the night or under adverse weather, enabling the pilot to find his way without visual navigation. A device for precision blind bombing, called X–Geräte (made up of two basic radio devices: FuG 22 and FuG 17X), was based on it. This automatic system worked on the principle of radio wave reception from two transmitters which created two lines that crossed on the target (the system is known as Wotan I). One of the lines was the bomber's path, the other identified the bomb dropping point. Using this system a single crew (or more, but at intervals) took off from a base in France and, maintaining radio contact with a radio station at Cherbourg, entered the radio path transmitted by this station which led them straight to the target. 50 km before the target, the bomber passed the first crossing of radio lines from the station at Cher-

bourg and another at Calais, which informed the crew that the target was approaching. The pilot steered the machine straight along the line of the Cherbourg signal, and the bombardier set to his computer made Cherbourg signal, and the bombardier sat to his computer made up of three clocks with three pointers, four pushbuttons and an additional clock to synchronise two of the above mentioned pointers. The bombardier started the clock on the second crossing, 30 km prior to the target. On the third he released the clock reading with a pushbutton, and started the automatic bomb release system. This ended the offensive role of the crew, and the next thing to do was to return to base leaving the way clear for another guided bomber, or a whole group homing in onto the fire caused by the first one. The X–Geräte allowed 90 m precision at a radius of 320 km. The Y–Geräte (made up of three basic radio devices: FuG 28 and FuG 17E) was a modification of the X–Geräte working on the same principle (the system is called Wotan II). The main difference was the new guidance system allowed greater precision, signal coding (which prevented the British from using efficient countermeasures) and full automation with (or without) the exception of the bomb release which could be triggered off by a signal from the ground or the last point signal in Morse code,

according to a set key of transmission. Essentially the Y–Geräte enabled the Heinkel to be guided from the ground with minimum interference from the crew, and bombing of a point target (like a railway station) from an altitude of not less than 6000 m at a distance of 200–250 km. The only shortcoming of the system was that it worked in the 42.1–47.9 MHz band (the X–Geräte — 70–74 MHz) which covered the radio band (45 MHz) used by a north London BBC station. The British discovered this quite quickly and 80 Wing (a secret RAF radio warfare unit) used this to intercept signals to and from the aircraft and jam them.

In the second half of 1940 the He 111H–3, H–4 and H–5, and the P sub-variants were subject to continuous modification: the armour, equipment (like dinghies) and armament. This led to the appearance of Heinkels with machine guns fixed in the tails, parallel to the fuselage axis (at least in the machines manufactured since about October); machine guns above the forward gunnerRs position and, in some series, slightly modified MG FF pods under the central fuselage. This weapon had great firepower, but its usefulness was limited because the defensive zone it covered was the least important. At that time the rearview mirrors, spherical windshields on the dorsal positions, and armour plate for upper gunners appeared on He 111s. During the same period some aircraft were fitted with tail mounted glider-towing mountings included in the Rfstsatz 2. In contrast to the quite rare, in this time, R2 modification, the K4U autopilot was fitted to all Heinkels from the very beginning of 1940. Another modification was connected with the return of the land-based torpedo aircraft concept, questioned in 1938. By 1940, however, thinking had changed and several aircraft of KG 26 were adapted to carry torpedoes on racks with their fairing removed, mounted under the wing centre section just outboard of the bomb doors. The torpedo-carrying He 111s were fitted with new bombsights, and the 'cigars' were released by the navigator, with use of a special makeshift device. Another makeshift modification was done in KG 55 where MG FF cannon were installed in the 'Ikaria' nacelles, instead of machine guns. The cannon and nacelles were fixed since the cannon recoil was too strong for the rotating mounting.

In the summer of 1940 and early 1941 two another factories modifications were produced too. There were anti-balloon protection — Kuto — and equippment for tropical service. The first was installed in all night bomber versions and was called marked — for example — He 111 H–3/kuto. This installation was made up of two „rasors" installed in the leading edge of wings, outside of engines. The second was introduced in all He 111 which were used in Africa and marked — for example — He 111 H–3/trop. This type of aircraft was equipped with special filters in engines, pylons and special covers for weapons. In the fuselage were installed special radio set and tanks with drinkwater for crew.

Heinkel He 111H–3, H–4 and H–5 models satisfied the needs of German bomber units during 1940. Their versatility was becoming legendary. The three versions satisfied Luftwaffe needs for various kinds of bombers, so there was nothing left to be desired, except a modern successor to the He 111. However, this wish could not be fulfilled. The bomber development programme was halted, and the Ju 88 failed to meet the hopes connected with it. This situation brought a new Heinkel variant, the He 111 H–6, intended as a stop-gap until the arrival of the new generation bombers. It seems that the designers had only one thing in mind when developing this aircraft — standardisation. The only new elements in this variant were the PVC 1006B pylons for torpedoes in the Rüstsatz C, or the new ETC 2000A for 2000 kg bombs and the wooden Junkers VS 11 propeller, with a broader blade, already introduced in small numbers in the later H–3 to H–5 versions. The aircraft had similar

It is not R–Gerät, but a Heinkel's HeS 001 turbojet engine. Another one was installed beneath opposite wing. This He 111H–1 is coded KC(G?)+HX.

(MVT via M. Krzyżan)

equipment and power plants to those of the later H–3, H–4 or H–5 (i.e. Jumo 211F–2) and the same armament (the first series used a machine gun in the forward position, replaced later by a 20 mm cannon). Only the internal systems were changed, and some skin panels in order to simplify the manufacturing process.

The He 111H–6 entered service with the Luftwaffe in early spring of 1941, gradually replacing the H–3 as well as the H–4 and H–5. Its front-line service was provisionally estimated to be a year, when it would be superseded by another, more modern bomber. As things turned out, the H–6 remained in service until 1943, only to be replaced by ... another He 111 variant! The He 111H–6 was an extremely versatile machine that could carry out both strategic and tactical tasks. It could be a bomber (night or day, short or long range), torpedo-carrier, mine-layer, heavy and night fighter, attack, reconnaissance, transport or liaison aircraft. The He 111H–6 was manufactured in greater numbers than any other version of the Gfnter brothers design.

The next seven Heinkel versions that followed fall into two categories; one is the aircraft that were in fact slightly modified H–6s, with external or internal difference, which did not phase out their predecessor from service, the other consists of the specialised variants. The first included the He 111H–7, H–9 and H–10, all developed in 1941, (the first two not being introduced into service; while the second category included the He 111H–12, H–14 and H–15 (H–6-based) and the H–11 (H–10-based).

The He 111 H–8 based on earler H–4 and H–5 versions. This special, a night bomber model, was developed early in 1941, and differed from other variants in anti-barrage balloon protection known as 'Seilsprengpatrone Klette' or shorter 'Klette Gerat'. In the H–8 this was made up of two long angled bars, fixed to the fuselage and wings via special struts. At the end of the wings special cutting devices, called 'Kuto-Nase', were fitted which would cut the balloon line after it slipped there along the projecting structure. The whole system, elaborated in an AVA firm at Gottingen and was rather impractical, and rendered the He 111 useless as a bomber. It reduced the top speed dramatically, added much extra weight as it weighed more than 250 kg and required a similar weight to be placed in the rear fuselage to keep the CG correct, affected manoeuvrability, made flying the aircraft difficult and reduced bomb load to 1000 kg. Such a machine was only armed with two guns (dorsal and ventral), and manned by a crew of four. As can be seen from the above this model was a highly specialised modification, and not a practical one for combat units, so after a brief career all the surviving aircraft (more than 20 out of 30) were demodified and, under the designation of He111H–8/R2, handed to transport units [13], where they were used for glider towing.

The experience with the H–8 led to the creation in the autumn 1941 of the more useful, and longer produced, H–10 which was a standard night bomber, fitted with the Kuto (in wings) and a Kuto-Nase at the cockpit. The new Kuto-Nase device was simply horizontal reinforcing bar on the cockpit framing for protection from the effect of hitting a line. The bomber survival factor for collisions with balloon lines fell from 95% for the H–8 to 35% for the H–10, but the latter was a fully capable bomber. Very often they also had fire dampers fitted on the forward firing cannon. Moreover this version introduced emergency fuel jettisoning from the wing tanks and, some time later, the FuG 101 radar altimeter which soon became standard on all night versions of the He 111. An additional novelty was the completely enclosed, and well armoured dorsal gunnerRs position, armed with a 13 mm MG 131 gun, and the Peil EZ–6 radio finder which replaced the Peil G5.

Just after H–10 manufacturing started, another version called H–11 entered production. This was a specialised H–10 modification, with a

The He 111H–12/15 (or simply — the He 111H without ventral pod) with the Heinkel's HeS 011 turbojet engine beneath fuselage. The tests were completed in 1942.

(MVT via M. Krzyżan)

new PVC pylon that resembled a Vtable topR with 20 bomb rack 'fingers' which enabled carriage of five 250 kg bombs. The pylon was so designed that with little work it could accept new arrangement of racks for even three e.g. 1000 kg bombs.

Just like in the late H–10s, the upper gun position was totally enclosed, well armoured with reinforced glass and armed with a 13 mm MG 131 gun, while the ventral position received the twinned MG 81Z. This was better than the MG 15 or MG 17, since it had higher rate of fire (by 400 rounds per minute over the MG 17, and by 550 rounds pm over the MG 15). A little later similar modification was made in the side positions, replacing the old MG 17 with the new MG 81, and in the H–11/R1 variant, even the MG 81Z, thus increasing the total number of guns in an He 111 to eight, plus a cannon. Like in other similar versions with external pylons, this too accommodated a 835 litre fuel tank in the fuselage. Some aircraft of this variant were also

fitted with Kuto-Nase, Kuto and FuG 101, like in the H–10.

At the beginning of the 1940s, the Luftwaffe carried out tests of many remotely controlled airborne weapon systems. Their main aim was to destroy large, even moving targets at a distance which would protect their own crews from losses. Several bomber types were used for the tests, and later entered service, and the He 111 was the first of these. Flying bomb and torpedo trials (with Bv 246, Bv 143, L–10, Hs 293 and FX) had already been carried out on He 111Es adapted for that role, but for the experimental VVersuchsstaffel 293R a special series of He 111H–12s was built. This modification, in the planned combat configuration, was to differ in the lack of the ventral gunner's cupola, the removal of nose cannon and modified radio-bomb aiming equipment in the front cockpit (among others the FuG 203b Kehl III bomb guidance transmitter for the Hs 293); two attachments under the wing centre section and, probably, additional fuel tanks. However, in

This same aircraft as above — interrior of bomb bays was adopted as laboratorium for testing turbojet engines.

(MVT via M. Krzyżan)

effect this machine was useless operationally because of insufficient service ceiling, and so the whole quantity manufactured between 1941 and 1943, at most some 50 aircraft, were used for training purposes, with all their defensive armament removed. The H–12 was replaced in front-line units with the Do 217 and He 177. Apart from the He 111H–12, there was another variant, called He 111H–15, to carry another airborne flying weapon, the Bv 246. This had three attachments for these bombs, two under the wings and one under the port forward fuselage. Testing of this weapon type revealed that it did not satisfy requirements and the existing aircraft were rebuilt for other duties (probably to the H–12 standard or as glider tugs). The H–15 series did not otherwise differ from the H–12, apart from slightly changed internal equipment and the form and position of pylons.

In the autumn of 1940, during the Blitz, the Luftwaffe introduced new bombing tactics which consisted in destroying point targets with large bombs, or marking large area targets by the best crews. To ease such tasks the aircraft were fitted with special electronic equipment — described above — which directed the pilot and let the bombardier release bombs at a signal from the ground. Aircraft equipped with X– or Y–Geräte served until 1942, but earlier on the RLM decided to order a single series of some 100 aircraft fitted with equipment including FuG 25, FuG 351 (probably in the place of Peil G 5) and modified X–Geräte (or Y–Geräte, or FuG 120) which made up a new type of guiding system called Wotan III. The aerial arrangement on the fuselage was probably the very similar as on the X–Geräte equipped machines, and the only distinguishing point was the ventral cupola, new propeller blades and other minor details changed with respect to the H–3x. The 30 He 111H–14s built were delivered to two units: the Sonderkommando Rastedter (based on KG 40) which acted in the Western Europe, and KG 100 flying over the Eastern Front and Mediterranean, while a further 70 aircraft were scattered among other units (e.g. KG 66) or converted to normal bombers or glider tugs. They were succeeded in production by the electronic warfare variant of the He 111H–16, which was simpler, and easier in operation. The new model was developed at the beginning of 1942 as the successor for the H–6. The basic difference between this, and the earlier versions, lay in the modified internal installations, construction process and new modifications introduced in the H–10 to H–15 models. The bomb combination was identical to that of the H–6, 1 – 2 tonnes externally and 1 tonne internally, whereas in the overload mode it could carry up to 3000 kg of bombs, but this required a good runway or two R–Gerat rocket boosters under wings. These were started during the take-off run, and after the take-off and gaining sufficient height they finished operation and were parachuted to the ground.

The basic difference with respect to preceding models, which was a technological revolution, was the fact that construction was changed so as to enable numerous modifications without much work. The factory-fresh aircraft were in four basic variants of this model: the standard one; the H–16/R1, equipped with DL 131 gun turret mounted dorsally in place of the upper station, and two MG 81Z guns in the side windows; the R2, a tug; and the R3, a pathfinder bomber, successor of the He 111H–14. A high degree of commonality was thus reached which enabled intermittent manufacture of small series of the specialized R3 variant in between long series of standard bombers. The orders were fulfille quickly since no extra time at all was required to prepare the airframe for fitting of the radio-navigation systems. It was sufficient to order the radio sets and install them in the forthcoming batch of Heinkels, using pre-prepared attachments in the fuselage. The same operation could be carried out at field workshops. All the mentioned Rustsatzes were made up of various equipment elements which composed a standard sets. There were included various fuel tanks and fuel systems (B–Rüstsatze), weapons systems (W–Rüstsatze), bomb pylons (M–Rüstsatze) and electronic equipment.

A little later, additional modifications were applied to the radio system, the FuG X wireless set being replaced by the FuG 16ZY, and the Fubl 1 with the Fubl 2, the latter covered with an additional plastics fairing. Typical electronic sets were not sufficient in 1943/44, so a new electronic warfare Heinkel was developed with radar equipment. This model was fitted with the latest technology, the FuG 200 air-surface radar. These sets were mainly installed in the H–18 short series variant of the He 111, but also were used on H–16 and probably H–20 too. Like in other similar versions, the H–18 with radar crew numbered six, offensive armament was reduced max. up to 2000 kg. This variant is easily recognisable by the wealth of radar aerials protruding out of the cockpit. These highly specialised machines were not built in quantity, the majority being sent to the Western Europe-based KG 40, some to the bomber units of the Eastern Front.

The He 111H–18 had all the H–16 Rüstsatz modifications, but it was not manufactured in series like other models, but rather modified with new innovations from other versions to the H–18 standard, as was the case with the H–8 or H–14.

At the middle of 1943 another version of the He 111 came into production, which would summarise the experience, technological development and go one step further towards a fully versatile aircraft. Three prototypes were used to develop this variant, the He 111 V46, V47 and V48. The interior was so designed as to accept

equipment kits to make it: a paratroop transport for 16 men or two 800 kg supply pods on external racks, strengthened weapons (the H–20/R1 model); a glider tug (R2); a bomber with extended radio-navigational equipment (R3); and a night intruder bomber (R4). the differences between individual variants were little and practically limited to the armament. The transport version was manned by three men, of whom two were gunners operating 13mm guns (forward and dorsal), but the forward gun was often removed, while the side guns were left to be manned by the paratroops. The R1 model had stronger armament of three 13mm guns (one in the nose, in the place of the MG FF cannon), and two MG 81Z in side stations, the R4 had racks for twenty 50 kg bombs fitted internally instead of the previous ESAC 250 adaptors and additional armour. All models were produced in the night-bomber version. Many sources claimed say that there was a new element in the H–20/R4, the GM 1 system installation that permitted a short-time power boost at high altitudes by injecting a water-methyl mixture into the cylinders. If it is a truth, the GM 1 tank was installed in one of the bomb bays. All He 111H–20 models featured a dorsal gun turret. Very few H–20s were equipped with the FuG 220 'Lichtenstein' SN-2 radars intended for use in the aviation schools and fighter units of the Eastern Front. There, they were used in a role similar too today's AWACS.

Since 1939/1940 the He 111 H and P variants were produced in no less than five another versions known as Umrüst – Baustatz. The first one was a disposal version for staff officers, the next a reconnaissance model, another was a ground attack/fighter version with additional weapons — 2 x MG 151/20 in the fuselage and next 2 MG 151 (or MG 81) under the port wing — and the aircraft with radar (FuG 200 and FuG 220) sets were built in this system too. In 1944 on the base of disposal model was built another Umrüst, a transport version.

The He 111H–21 was the last development version of the Gfnter brothers design. It differed from its predecessor in the new Jumo 213 E-1 engines, rated at 1750 hp (1290 kw), which allowed it to reach the VfascinatingR speed of 480 km/h, an altitude of 10000 m and an increase in the bomb load to 3000 kg. Apart from that the aircraft was practically unchanged from its predecessor. The haste with which it went into production resulted in the first 22 aircraft being finished as H–20/R3 with Jumo 211 F–2 engines since the delivery of Jumo 213 E–1's was late. Total number of the He 111H–21's produced is not known, but could not exceed 200 aircraft.

In the late spring of 1944 the Germans were forced to build a new variant of the He 111, this time a carrier for Fi 103 (V–1) flying bombs. Based on the experience gained with the He

The transport version of the He 111H–20/R2 model or — as it is identified — He 111H–23 with Jumo 213 engines. It is painted overall black.

14

111H–12 and H–15, the Heinkel design office worked out a system of attaching one Fi 103 under the wing centre section on the ETC 2000 pylon on the port or starboard side of the fuselage. As from the end of summer 1944 the Heinkel 111s were no longer in production, these new tasks were carried out by aircraft previously detached from the production line or coming back to the factory for 'rejuvenation'. The only visual mark was a small detail on the fuselage side through which a wire passed connecting the bombRs engine with the panel of the radio-operator who launched the bomb at the navigator's signal. The H–22 was mainly modified from the H–20 variant, so it is only possible to determine whether a certain aircraft was a H–22 if a photograph was taken before the Fi 103 was released. Apart from the FuG 217 R 'Neptun' warning radar, the machines were also equipped with an FuG 101 radio-altimeter.

The last model, the He 111H–23 was a special duties transport, powered with Jumo 213 A–1 engines, rated at 1755 hp (1305 kw). The aircraft, with a crew of four, was based on the transport version of the He 111H–16 and could accommodate eight commandos with their equipment in the bomb compartment. Few Heinkels of the H–23 version were manufactured, and KG 200 being their principal user. The He 111H–23 ends the 'Flying Spade' story. During nine years of service 32 production versions were developed, and these were manufactured in varying numbers. The second generation of the bomber, the H and P variants, were much more numerous, with 22 variants, of which 17 were Hs.

The output figures for the second generation are as follows: 1938 – 1399 aircraft; 1940 – 827; 1941 – 930; 1942 – 1337; 1943 –1408; and 1944 –714. Altogether 6615 aircraft of the H and P versions were manufactured. Moreover, 236 He 111H–16s were built in the 1940s at the CASA factory at Seville in Spain, but it is not true that any He 111Rs were produced in Rumania. The total number of Heinkel 111s manufactured between 1936 and 1948 did not exceed 7800 aircraft (combat, civil; and prototypes). One He 111 standard model, cost in 1940 265,650 Reichsmark, including 61,750 Rm for engines. One He 111 was 30,650 Rm more expensive than a Do 17, and 39,300 Rm less expensive than a Ju 88.

Special versions

The most intriguing and extraordinary version of the Günter brothers bomber, developed in 1941, was a combination of two He 111s into one five-engined heavy glider tug. Work on this Heinkel model was started early in 1941, when the Ju 322 and Me 321 gliders were already about to be first flown. Both gliders were developed for the anticipated invasion of Britain in 1940 and were designed in such a hurry that no one thought of a suitable towing aircraft. This problem was neglected and it was proposed that older Bf 110s would be used for that purpose, but this

aircraft were too small for the purpose, and no less than three were needed to tow a Me 321 Gigant such an arrangement causing many problems and requiring excellent and patient pilots. The troubles caused by this solution were obvious to General E. Udet who, during one of his visits to Heinkel, suggested quick modification of the He 111 so that it could tow the giant gliders. Even though the changes were to be quick and cheap, bringing it to serviceable stage took three months. After that period, two prototypes were sent to Rechlin where they earned very favourable opinions. In the winter of 1941 the Marienehe factory started assembly of the first five machines, based on ten [14] He 111H–6s, and the next batch was manufactured during winter-spring 1942, using ten He 111H–16s. All the aircraft reached Luftwaffe units by the end of the spring.

Since the power of four engines was insufficient, the designers decided to connect the two fuselages with an additional central wing which enclosed fuel tanks, flaps, and a fifth Jumo 211 F–2 engine. The machine was still easy to fly and disposed the excess power necessary to tow ten – tonne gliders. The crew consisted of seven (instead of ten in two standard He 111s), including two pilots in two separate cockpits, with one of these (the co-pilot) responsible also for navigation. Their job was the most difficult, especially during take-off and landing. Synchronising engine and undercarriage operation required much Heinkel experience, and above all, good co-operation of the pilots, since each controlled 'his' landing gear and 'his' engines (the skipper two, the co-pilot three).

The aircraft weighed some 14 tonnes, and the AUW (with standard fuel) was 20 tonnes. With four extra tanks it could stay airborne for 10 hours while towing one Me 321 or three Go 242 over 4000 km. To facilitate taking off form advanced landing strips the He 111Z could accept four R–Geräte devices. It could stay airborne even with only 3 engines working, and level flight was even possible on two engines.

The He 111Z succeeded in difficult field conditions so that the RLM staff proposed in 1944 the development of the He 111Z–2 long-range bomber and Z–3 reconnaissance plane. The former was to carry 7000 kg bombs over a distance of 4000 km, and the latter to photograph targets even as distant as 6000 km away. Both ideas were irrational, however, both for economical and military reasons.

One of the main shortcomings of the He 111 was its low service ceiling of only 6000 m. This was to become less important in 1943, when new bombers were to enter service, but when this proved impossible, a high-altitude Heinkel model was suggested.

This was at first attempted by modifying production Jumo 211F engines with turbo-supercharger and a new cooling system, but tests proved the idea was not right. This led to abandoning the He 111R–1 and concentrating, from early 1944, on the He 111R–2, powered with DB 603s, rated at 1785 hp. These engines had Hirth or TKL 15 turbo-superchargers built-in thanks to which the aircraft could reach 500 km/h at 14000 m. The testing was started with the He 111 V32 prototype, powered with DB 601U engines with TK 9AC superchargers, but unsatisfactory results led to cancellation of the high-altitude He 111 programme.

NOTES:

[1] It is worth noting here that there were no such objections against the Ju 86B/C/Z, 47 of which were manufactured, even though it also could only carry 10 passengers. This suggests that the economic shortcomings of the civil He 111 was not the real problem.

[2] After WWII the War-Pac airlines used cost-ineffective Soviet aircraft for similar reasons.

[3] The number of 500 bombers might seem small today, but it should be remembered that in the thirties many of Germany's neighbours possessed a smaller total number of all combat aircraft.

[4] RVM – Reichsverkehrsministerium – Reich's Ministry of Transport, in 1935 renamed RLM – Reichsluftfahrtministerium – Reich's Ministry of Aviation

[5] H. Nowarra 'Die He 111'; Stuttgart 1979, P.48

[6] B. Philpott 'German bombers over England', Cambridge 1978, p.17

[7] Nowarra/Green. The V11 could indeed be used for testing of the Jumo 213 A–3 but this would have had to happen much later (summer – autumn 1938?).

[8] Probably the He 111V6 was not the prototype He 111E, but it is also difficult to assume assume the V10 was.

[9] Probably this prototype had already been used to develop the F–4 which, (according to Nowarra), was also made with torpedo units in mind.

[10] According to Green these were DB 600 CG engines, according to Nowarra the DB 601 Aa, according to Leistungstabelle der Deutschen Kriegsflugzeuge, Stand 1.12.1938, DB 600C. In the author's opinion these could not be other than DB 600G or Ga since at that time these types were used and it would make no sense to use less powerful units (C or CG) if more powerful versins were available.

[11] The first series were powered with the D–1 version.

[12] In 1941 the Y–Geräte was also installed in He 111 H – 6s.

[13] Since 1941 it was a standard practice to deliver some batches of Heinkel 111's to glider units, and since 1942 to transport's. The aircraft withdrawn from the front-line went to flying schools where they were sometimes converted to trainers, or to glider units after installing a towing device. From about 1941 the factory fresh He 111/R2s were delivered directly to combat and then transport units.

[14] According to other sources only 10 He 111Zs were built, 2 prototypes, 3 H–6-based, and 5 H–16-based.

A well known photo of a He 111Z, 0G + B(D?)..., with auxiliary fuel tanks, 900 litres capacity each. This plane is probably from LLG 1, photographed in winter 1943, in the Southern Russia (West of Stalingrad or Krim). Note a MG FF cannon in the left cockpit and a MG 131 in the right one.

(MVT via M. Krzyżan)

EKSPORT

CHINA

Even before the Heinkels with German crews took part in the Spanish Civil War, the type had already been in combat with the Chinese Air Force.

At the time when Ernst Heinkel Flugzeugwerke was in serious trouble, following rejection of their aircraft, the Chinese military mission was in Germany, looking for weaponry to equip their army, fighting Japanese aggression. German authorities received them gladly, and allowed Heinkel to get rid of six He 111As. All six were dispatched in crates from Hamburg in mid-1936, and arrived in China at the end of the year. After a short 'acquaintance' period they went to the 19th Heavy Bomber Squadron within the 8th Group. Their debut was a complete failure, however. During one of their first missions near Shanghai, in the company of 6 Martin 139s and escorted by Boeing 281s they were intercepted by Japanese fighters, and out of five He 111s only three returned to base. The type was still in service with the 19th Squadron in the early autumn of 1937, and the last machine was shot down in error by Chinese student pilot, probably in 1939.

RUMANIA

Following closer cooperation with Germany, the Rumanian Army was subjected to German training programmes, and supplied with German weapons. Among others, the FARR — Fortele Aeriene Regale Romane — (Royal Air Force of Rumania) received 32 He 111Hs in 1940 in exchange for petrol. 27 of these were immediately taken on strength of Escadrila (flights) 78, 79 and 80 of the Grupul 5 Bombardament (5th Bomber Group) which attained operational capability in the spring of the following year. All the He 111s received from the Germans were old machines after a general overhaul which brought them up to the H–3 standard of second part 1940. From June 22, 1941 the flights were continuously in action, forming the backbone of the Rumanian bomber force. The losses during training and fighting were only replaced in 1942 with another batch 30 aircraft, among them 9 of the H–6 variant. The He 111s remained in service until August 1944 when, during the political storm, many aircraft were destroyed or captured by the Soviets. The remains of Grupul 5 were reorganised into one unit with 7 He 111s and 10 Ju 88s which became a part of the 1st Rumunskiy Smyeshanniy Avyatsyonniy Korpus numbering 113 aircraft, acting under the command of the Soviet 5th Vozdushnaya Armia (5th Aviation Army).

HUNGARY

Representatives of the MKHL — Magyar Kiralyi Honved Legiero — (Royal Hungarian Army Air Force) [1] made efforts to purchase 40 He 111s as early as the summer of 1940, but (probably because Rumanian pressure) the contract was not signed and the Hungarians had to content themselves with two transport He 111s. Only in 1941 were they able to buy another 8 He 111P–6s, equipped for transport duties, with deliveries at the turn of 1941, and another batch of 5 He 111P–2s was delivered in 1942. The last He 111P–2 was taken on the strength of the Hungarian forces in 1944, thereby increasing the total number to 16 aircraft.

Two He 111Ps out of six possessed were transferred for a short period in the spring of 1942 from the MKHL command transport flight to the 1/1 Távolfelderítő század (1st Long Range Reconnaissance Flight), where they were used for training while awaiting He 111s deliveries from Germany. Even though the 1/1 Tf.Sz. was a reconnaissance flight, it won its fame in Hungary as a fighter unit. Between June 29 and August 13, 1942, in five combats with Soviet fighters, five Hungarian crews shot down 12 enemy aircraft ! In October 1942 the unit returned to Kursk where it started its 1942 summer campaign. In

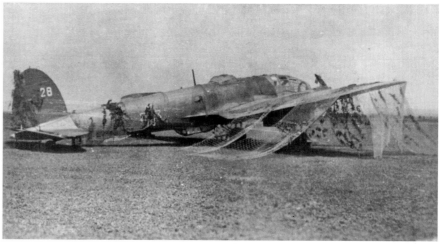

Above: One of the Rumanian He 111H–3 at an Ukrainian airfield. The aircraft is without DF-loop and armament, and it was probably used for VIP transport.
(Dénes Bernàd coll.)

A beautiful photo of a He 111H No.32 in the makings of FARR. Note a yellow strip on the tail and wingtips, there are also darker spots under the wing's crosses.
(Dénes Bernàd coll.)

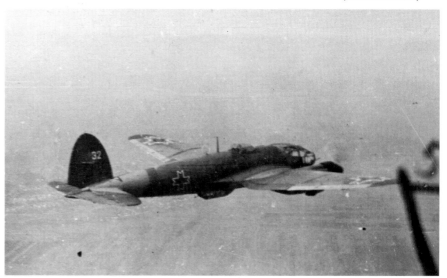

1943 the Heinkels were replaced by Junkers Ju 88Ds. The remaining He 111s were used for transport and liason duties until the end of the war.

SLOVAKIA

The SVZ — Slovenske Vzdusne Zbrane (Slovakian Air Force) started the war on the German side with 6 Letkas (flights) equipped with indigenous types of aircraft and it was not until 1943 that a major reorganisation took place, which amongst other things led to the creation of the 41 Bombova Letka (Bomber Flight) which had — apart from 7 SM. 84s — 3 He 111Hs. the unit was used in the fighting over Kuban in summer of 1943. The 51 Dopravni Letka (transport Flight) was formed in Slovakia which also received (among others) a single He 111H (coded S–81) that was mainly used as a VIP transport. This was soon followed by another He 111 (S–82) which was also used for paratroop training. After the war several He 111s were found at Czech and Slovak airfields (including one modified to H–12, or a standart combat H without the ventral pod lost in an accident). In

A CASA 2111 (i.e. He 111H–16 made in Spain), photographed just after the war. Note a English fashion D/F-loop type. The aircraft is not armed.
(IDHYCA via R. Michulec)

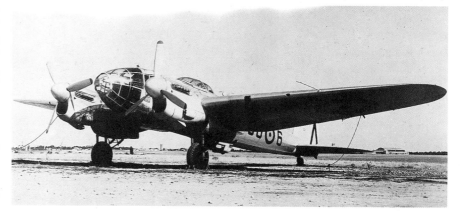

The Hungarian He 111P–6 coded F.7 + O6 from the long recce unit 1/1Tf.Sz., winter 1942/43, Kursk.

(G. Punka coll. via D. Bernàd)

1946 these were taken into service with Czechoslovak Air Force under the type designation LB–77. They served to train the flying personnel, e.g. in the 25 Letecky Pluk (Air Regiment). Available publications say the SVZ He 111s were of the H–10 variant, but in fact at least two of these were the early H versions (H–1/early H–6).

SPAIN

During the Spanish Civil War Germany supplied no less than 96 He 111s there, but in fact the real number could have reached 100. This supposition is based on the fact that 37 He 111s were lost during the war, which leaves 59 aircraft, which is only one more than the number in service with the Ejercito del Aire — AdE (Spanish Air Force) in March of 1940, a year after the war had ended. It seems improbable, however, that during a year of reorganisation and personnel training only one aircraft was lost in an accident.

All the Heinkels left in the Iberian Peninsula (59 – ~ 63 airplanes) were transferred after the war to the EdA in which the following units were formed, or converted to the type: Grupo 10–G–25, under the command of Antonio Rudeda Ureta (formed in August of 1938); Grupo 11–G–25, under the command of Ricardo Guerrero Lopez (formed in February of 1939); both within the 8a Escuadra of Eugenio Frutos Dieste. In the summer of 1940 the EdA was reorganised and all the 58 Heinkels were grouped in Regimentos 14 and 15, based at Zaragoza and Logroso. In 1943 the Spanish authorities started negotiations with Germany, regarding purchase of 50 He 111Hs and licence-production of the type for the EdA. The RLM agreed and a contract was signed eventually for 70 He 111H–16s and licence for some 130 more, to be built in the Construccions Aeronauticas S.A. at Tablada near Seville under the designation CASA 2111. The aircraft left the factory in three basic variants; bomber (CASA 2111A, A–1 and A–3), reconnaissance (CASA 2111C–1, C–2 and C–3) and transport (CASA 2111F and F–1). At the end of 1940s, the EdA headquarters decided to modify these bombers with more powerful engines. 173 Rolls–Royce 500–20 and 500–29 engines, rated at 1600 HP, were purchased in Britain. Engine replacement and modification was done gradually on the best 70 aircraft (between 1953 and 1956) and their designations were changed respectively to CASA 2111B (bomber), CASA 2111D (reconnaissance) and 2111E (transport). All the EdA

He 111s recieved new military designations introduced after WW.II:
He 111B/E B–2 — bomber
He 111B/E MB–2 — weather reconnaissance
CASA/He 111H–16 B–2 — bomber, Jumo engines
CASA/He 111H–16 BR–2H — reconnaissance, Jumo engines
CASA/He 111H–16 T–8 — transport, Jumo engines
CASA/He 111H–16 B–2I — bomber, RR engines
CASA/He 111H–16 BR–2I — reconnaissance, RR engines
CASA/He 111H–16 T–8B — transport, RR engines.

TURKEY

In 1937 representatives of the THK — Türk Hava Kuvvetleri (Turkish Air Force) agreed with Heinkel A.G. and the RLM as to the purchase of a small number of He 111 bombers, but under the condition that these be the latest model, rather than the He 111D on offer. The RLM decided to accept the condition and the He 111F–1 with new wing and DB 600 CG engine, was put into production. The first machine (D – AAAF) left the Oranienburg Factory in late/mid October 1937 and was delivered to Eskisehiw in Turkey by air. The remaining 23 aircraft were delivered there by the end of the year. Early in 1938 three boluks (companies) — equivalent to flights — of the 1nci alay (1st Regiment) were armed with all the Heinkels purchased which served in the unit until mid-1944, when they were phased out of front-line tservice in favour of Martin Baltimores and transferred to flying schools. Together with combat He 111s THK also bought 5 civil version He 111 G–5s, which were used for liaison duties.

BULGARIA

Because of a direct danger of combat, in the autumn 1943 a reorganisation was started in the VVB — Vozdushniye Voyski Bulgari (Bulgarian Air Arm), which included the acquisition of He 111H–16 for disposal duties. This aircraft (serial number 161604) was a special gift from Germany for the tsar Boris III. The He 111 was handed over to the Bulgarians in November 1943, and together with the other it was allocated to the Kuriersko Yato (Courier Flight) of the VVB command, where it served mainly to carry

CAPTURED AIRCRAFT

The British were the first to capture a flyable He 111H. This was the He 111H–1 of 5/KG 26, forced to land on February 9, 1940. After the necessary repairs it was repainted and allocated to No.1426 Enemy Aircraft Flight which tested captured aircraft. This machine, serialled AW 177, flew until November 10, 1943, when it crashed. Another Heinkel was captured by 260 Squadron at Tripoli in 1943. It was coded HS – ? and served as a hack in this unit.

The Americans found a few He 111s at the Algiers airfields in the spring of 1943. Two of these were H's with the civil registrations D – ACLQ and D – APOW, painted RLM 02 Grau overall. Both belonged to a German institution supervising the demilitarization of France.

Their further fates remain unknown, but it seems they were used by the units that captured them. During the French campaign in 1944 American troops captured another He 111, this time an H–11/R2, probably of TGr 30, which was later taken to the USA.[2] There it received the designation of FE–1600 and was subject to tests, being abandoned later.

A truly great harvest was found after the war ended, when dozens of Heinkels fell into the hands of the Allies. In Denmark alone 10 serviceable He 111s of various variants were found. Not only ground units took their share. The famous 56th FG captured an He 111 H–20 (or H–23) which was painted black and taken on strength. It was coded HV – COW and received the 56's recognition colours.

The French also captured several He 111 after the war and used them in the Armee de l'Air until the late 1940's as transport and liaison aircraft. The Soviets also got their He 111s, albeit in another way. Their first Madchen came from the French in 1938. This was the He 111 B–1, 25.32 which force-landed behind the enemy lines in Spain on December 17, 1937. Subsequent aircraft were captured in 1941. One of these was used for a while by 4 Ground Attack Air Regiment, and the electrically operated cockpit window covers were most fascinating for them. Of the collection of more than a dozen He 111s most were captured at Stalingrad, including some old modifications of KGr zbV 5. Four of these, including two He 111E of this unit, were taken to Moscow and shown in a captured equipment display in 1943. Some 10 captured Ju 87s and He 111/R2s were handed over by the Stalingrad Front to the Rostov Glider Pilot School, where they served in glider and airplane pilot training. A German technician helped Senior Lieutenant 'Batya' Petrakov learn their handling.

An He 111 B–1, He 111 H–11 and He 111 H–6 were tested in NII VVS in 1938, 1943 and 1944 respectively, the latter coming from KG 53. Many captured Heinkels were used by the Soviets in their secret special duties units of NKVD to transport agents or communist activists or to tow gliders with supplies for partisans. During one of such missions a black He 111 without any markings was shot down over Karelia by Juutilainen, a Finnish ace, in 1942.

VIPs until 1947. The aircraft, bearing the registration LZ–XAG, was handed to the Czechoslovaks in early 1948 as a gift, the same as with two other He 111s which were captured by Soviets in Austria and then transfered to Bulgaria in May of 1945.

The He 111 of Slovak Air Force used for VIP transport. Note a late version of the ventral pod and Jumo 211A–1 engines of the He 111H–1 model.

(S. Androvic coll. via D. Bernàd)

NOTES:

[1] In Hungarian language is the word 'Honved', used since 1848, which means 'Defence Forces (Army)', but I used the simpler word — Army.

[2] This He 111 had a small number on the vertical tail, a style of marking which was used by transport He 111s. The H–11 version was very old by 1945 and was not used in combat units by this time

CAMOUFLAGE AND MARKINGS

All five initial He 111 prototypes, six He 111A–0s and the pre-series He 111B–0s were painted overall RLM 63 or RLM 02 which can be described as medium gray with a little green added (to give a slight greenish hue). For unknown reasons also almost all B–1s sent to Spain were so painted, while all B–2s and the remaining B–1s were cowered with a complex, four-colour disruptive splinter camouflage. Possibly for these same reasons the first He 111Bs sent to Spain were repainted with RLM 63 or 02 paint. The best example of this is the aircraft 25.3 piloted by von Moreau. The scheme used Dunkelbraun – RLM 61 (chocolate brown), Mittelgrün – RLM 62 (medium green), and Hellgrau – RLM 63 (light grey, although of a darker shade than that applied to the undersurfaces and with a slight greenish hue). The lower portion of the aircraft was painted Hellblau – RLM 65 (light blue). All the individual colours were in the form of angular fields with many sharp angles to tire the observer's eye and provide better camouflage thanks to contrasting colours.

With the new generation of Heinkels (the He 111H/P) the old camouflage pattern was at first adapted, but then it was decided to develop a completely new one, less demanding in terms of the work involved in painting, but no less efficient. After the first experiments with earlier colours when entire aircraft were covered with large areas of RLM 05 (a light sand/khaki shade), Dunkelbraun – RLM 61 and Mittelgrun RLM 62, a new scheme was adopted very similar to the previous one. The only difference lay in rejection of the contrasting colours in favour of new, dark green hues. So, starting from early 1939, the upper and side surfaces were painted Schwarzgrün – RLM 70 (Black green) and Dunkelgrün – RLM 71 (Dark green), the lower surfaces remaining unchanged. The scheme was generally considered to be satisfactory, and was used until the end of the war.

All the schemes were applied according to precise templates which, however, did occasionally vary, so a particular field could decrease or increase, the division lines between upper colours could change, or the border between upper and lower surfaces colours could move up or down (particularly in the RLM 65, 70, 71 camouflage between 1939 and 1941). Changing colour positions, like in the He 111V17, or other extraordinary modifications were extremely rare.

In the second half of 1940, during the night actions against England, the RLM 65 proved too bright for the night sky, so most units started to cover lower and side surfaces, as well as light areas of the markings, with matt black, removable paint. KG 55 went further with splendid patterns of black patches all over the top surfaces, and often repainted entire aircraft black. Such a system of black camouflage remained in the Luftwaffe until the end of the war and was widely used over Europe, Africa and the Soviet Union.

Actions in new areas forced He 111 users to revise the painting systems to provide better camouflage in a particular environment. E.g. the

The He 111 with factory white code letters. The upper parts of camouflage are very well visible on this photo.

(MVT via M. Krzyżan)

He 111s used in Africa were painted Sandgelb – RLM 79 (Sand yellow) overall, rarely applying any mottle or fields of other colours. The aircraft operating over Russia often applied large or small areas of light grey RLM 76 (or RLM 77) or grey RLM 02, or, occasionally, khaki (or sand) over the factory applied camouflage. The third case might involve paints from captured Soviet stocks, as well as the colours mixed in the field, so it is extremely difficult to precisely determine the exact shades used, particularly as sand, grey or light grey look almost identical on black-and-white photos, so in most cases it is not possible to verify the colour.

During winter periods the aircraft used in Soviet territory were painted almost entirely white to merge with the ground. Often, when fighting in spring or autumn conditions, the top surfaces were usually covered with patterns of white over the camouflage. In both cases the white paint was water-removable, so after a short period this disappeared or soiled. If the winter was not coming to an end, a new cover of white could be applied over the old one, giving fantastic patterns.

Standard He 111 markings consisted, until 1939, of small crosses applied on both sides of the fuselage, approximately half way between the wing trailing edge and the horizontal tail surfaces, and four more painted on upper and lower wing tips. These markings were completed by a red band bearing a black swastika on a white disc across the fin and rudder and a five character alphanumeric code. The two first digits denoted the parent unit and its location, the remaining three identified the crew and the unit. For example the code '32+B13' identified an aircraft of the second Geschwader – '2' – in the third air district (Luftkreise) – '3' – thus '32+' – flown by the crew of – let say – Hans Schmitt (B) of the last Staffel (3) in the first (1) Gruppe – thus '+B13'. Thus knowing the system, you

knew Hans Schmitt flew in I/KG 153 based somewhere near Dresden.

With the growth and reorganisation of the Luftwaffe a new and less cumbersome system was necessary. This led to the four–character codes that remained in use by all units except the fighters until the end of the war. Such a code, e.g. '6N+CP', denoted three basic things: the unit ('6N' meant KG 100), and the crew of Hans Schmitt (C) in the last Staffel of the second Gruppe – 'P'. This system was a little more complicated, as you had to remember what letter identified particular Staffel (in this case 'P' stood for the third Staffel of the second Group, i.e. 6 Staffel of the Geschwader), rather rather than the two digits denoting the number of Staffel and Gruppe openly as in the previous system. The letter 'C' of the particular crew, was often painted or outlined with the Staffel colour. It was for practical, rather than aesthetical reasons, since it was easier to identify the unit colour than to read the letter at a distance. For similar reasons of quick recognition of a particular Gruppe, in the summer of 1940 a system was adopted where the Stabsschwarmen aircraft had thick wide bands applied to their vertical tails and/or wing upper surfaces. One band meant I Gruppe, two – II, three – III. Such markings allowed the rest of the Gruppe's aircraft to recognise their assembly areas at a distance without the need to identify the code letters.

With the early war experience it was discovered that the aircraft were too difficult to recognise by friendly ground and air troops, so at first the national markings were enlarged (e.g. the KG 27 He 111s carried crosses the size of the whole wing chord!). Later quick identification bands were introduced. On the Russian front these were in yellow (lower wing surfaces, rear fuselage, engine cowlings), but in Africa this merged against the ground, so white bands were used there.

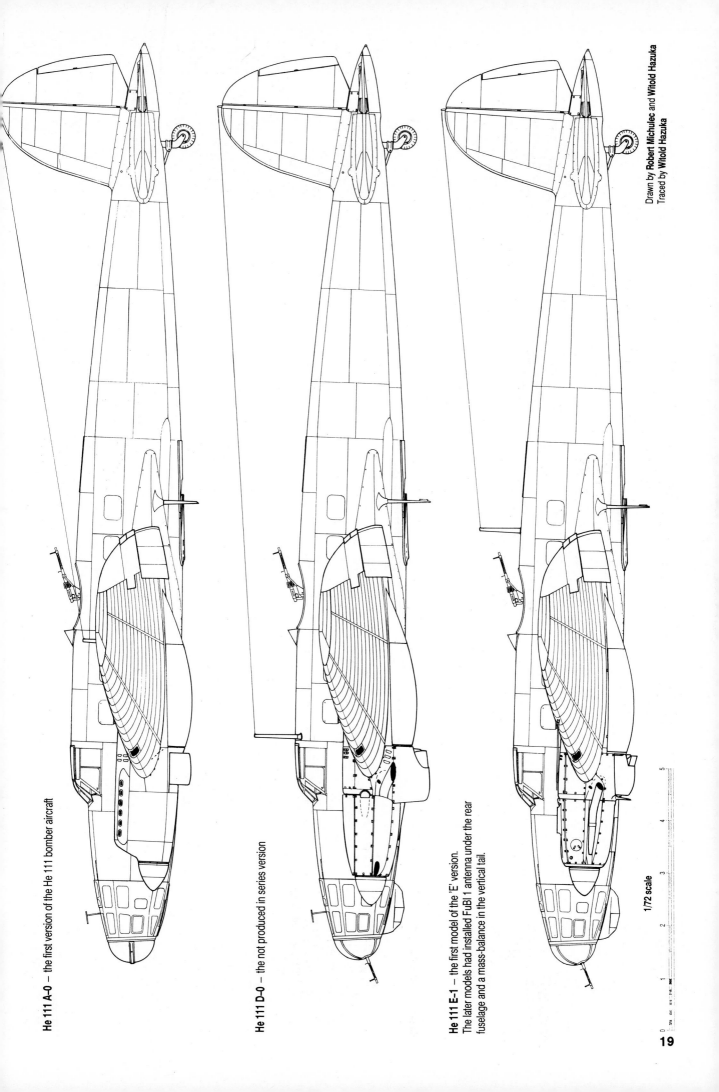

He 111 A-0 — the first version of the He 111 bomber aircraft

He 111 D-0 — the not produced in series version

He 111 E-1 — the first model of the 'E' version.
The later models had installed FuBl 1 antenna under the rear fuselage and a mass-balance in the vertical tail.

1/72 scale

Drawn by **Robert Michulec** and **Witold Hazuka**
Traced by **Witold Hazuka**

19

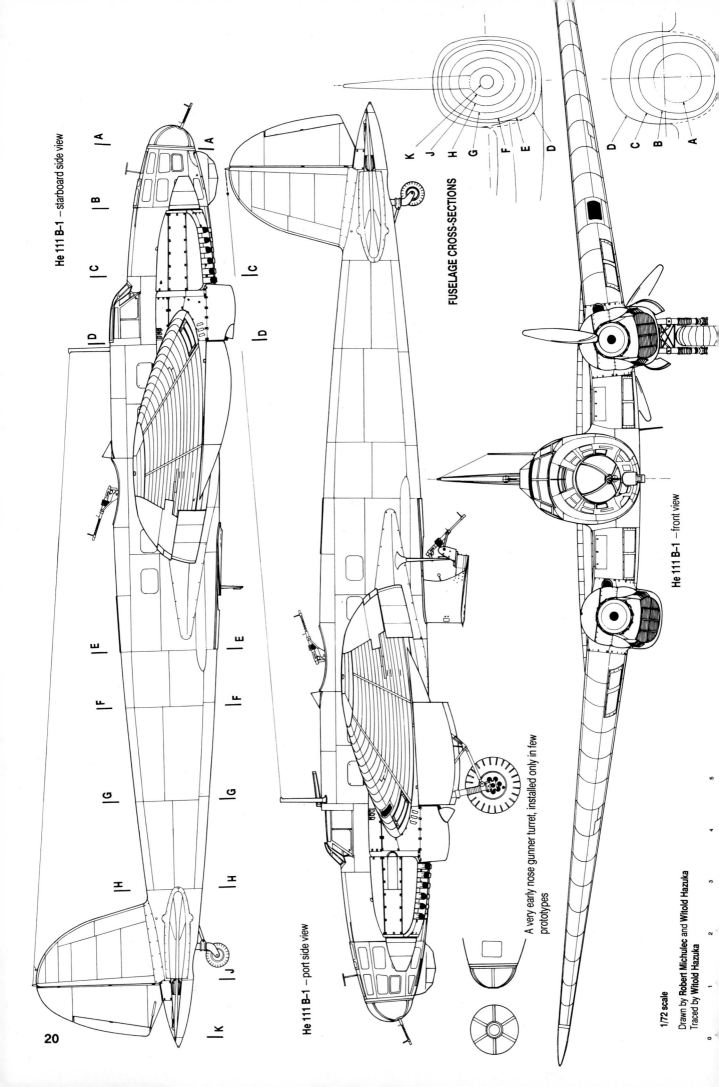

He 111 B-1 – starboard side view

He 111 B-1 – port side view

FUSELAGE CROSS-SECTIONS

He 111 B-1 – front view

A very early nose gunner turret, installed only in few prototypes

1/72 scale

Drawn by **Robert Michulec** and **Witold Hazuka**
Traced by **Witold Hazuka**

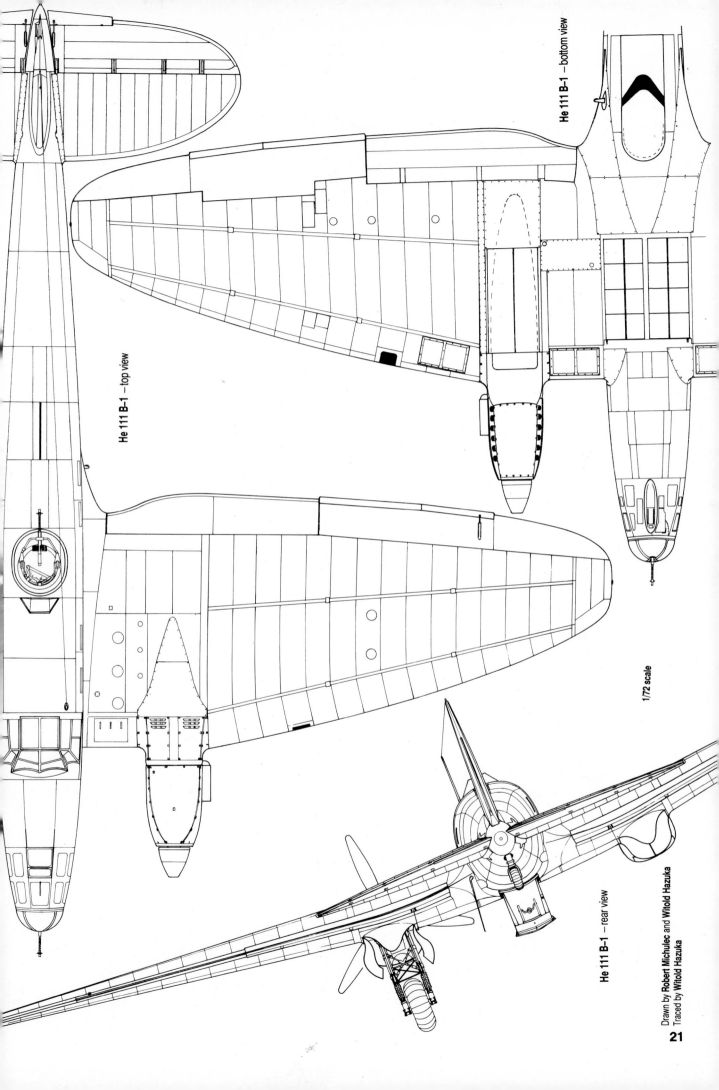

He 111 B-1 – bottom view

He 111 B-1 – top view

He 111 B-1 – rear view

1/72 scale

Drawn by Robert Michulec and Witold Hazuka
Traced by Witold Hazuka

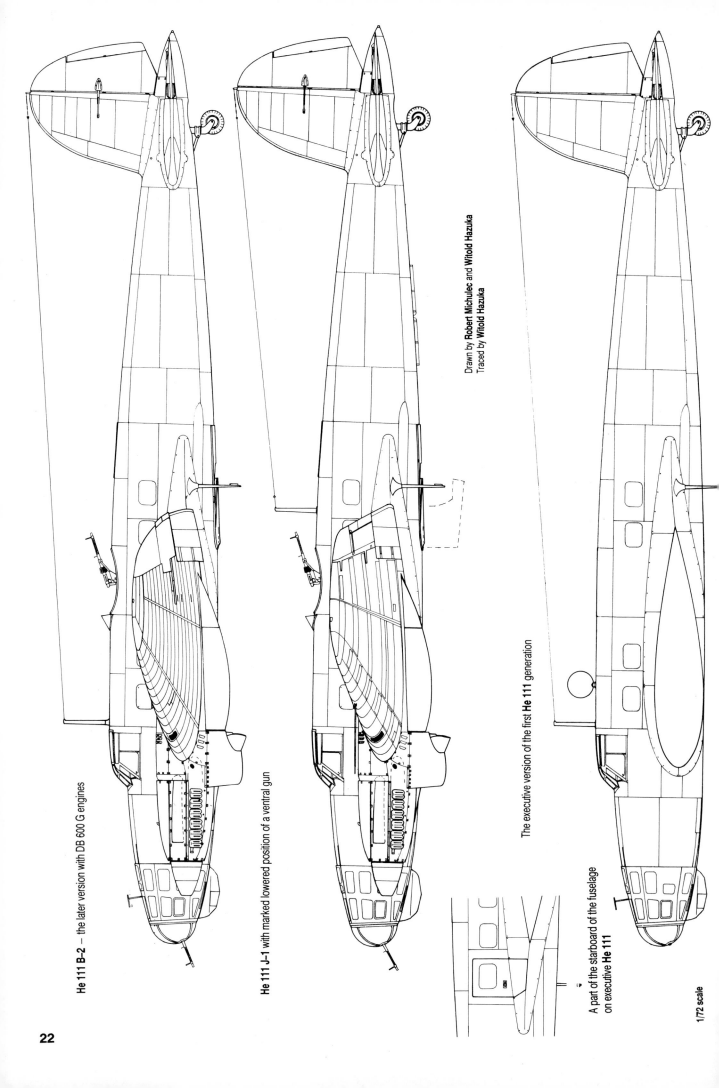

He 111 B-2 – the later version with DB 600 G engines

He 111 J-1 with marked lowered position of a ventral gun

Drawn by **Robert Michulec** and **Witold Hazuka**
Traced by **Witold Hazuka**

The executive version of the first **He 111** generation

A part of the starboard of the fuselage
on executive **He 111**

1/72 scale

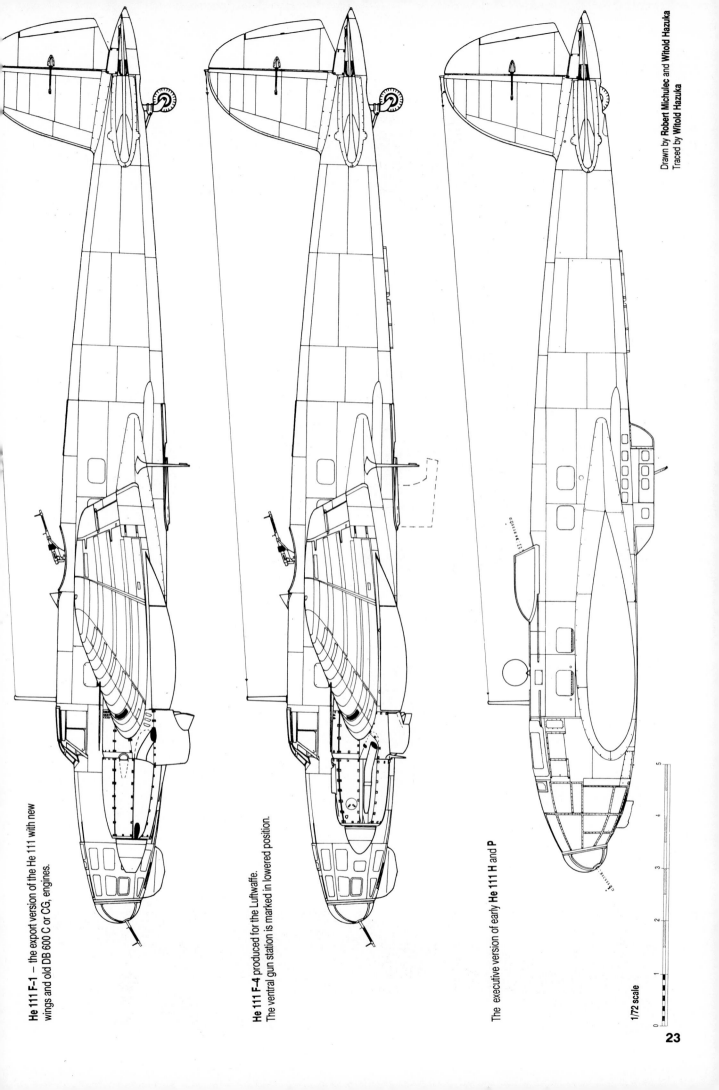

He 111 F-1 — the export version of the He 111 with new wings and old DB 600 C or CG, engines.

He 111 F-4 produced for the Luftwaffe.
The ventral gun station is marked in lowered position.

The executive version of early **He 111 H and P**

Drawn by **Robert Michulec** and **Witold Hazuka**
Traced by **Witold Hazuka**

1/72 scale

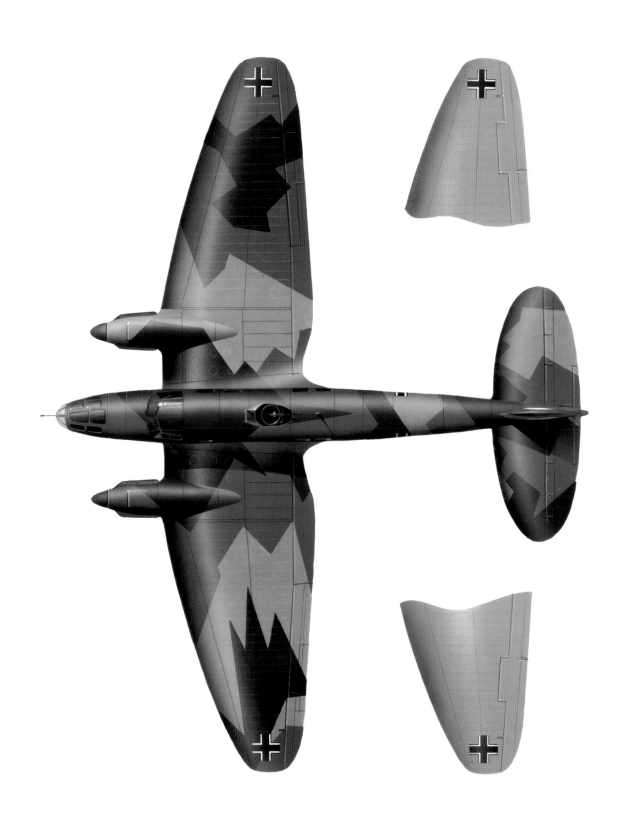

The emblem of the KG 1 „Hindenburg". The outline of the emblem was painted in the group colour (in this case green, the colour of staff flight of the KG 1).

The He 111E–3, coded V4+AB, of staff flight of I/KG1 Geschwader. The aircraft is camouflaged with RLM 61/62/63/65 colours and on the vertical tail has a swastika in the white circle on a red stripe – the emblem of the Third Reich. Just before the outbreak of the war this emblem was over-painted. During the war with Poland only a few of this version He 111's aircraft were used.

A pilot of the He 111 wearing a standard flying suit typical to the early period of the war.

Paint: Jarosław Wróbel

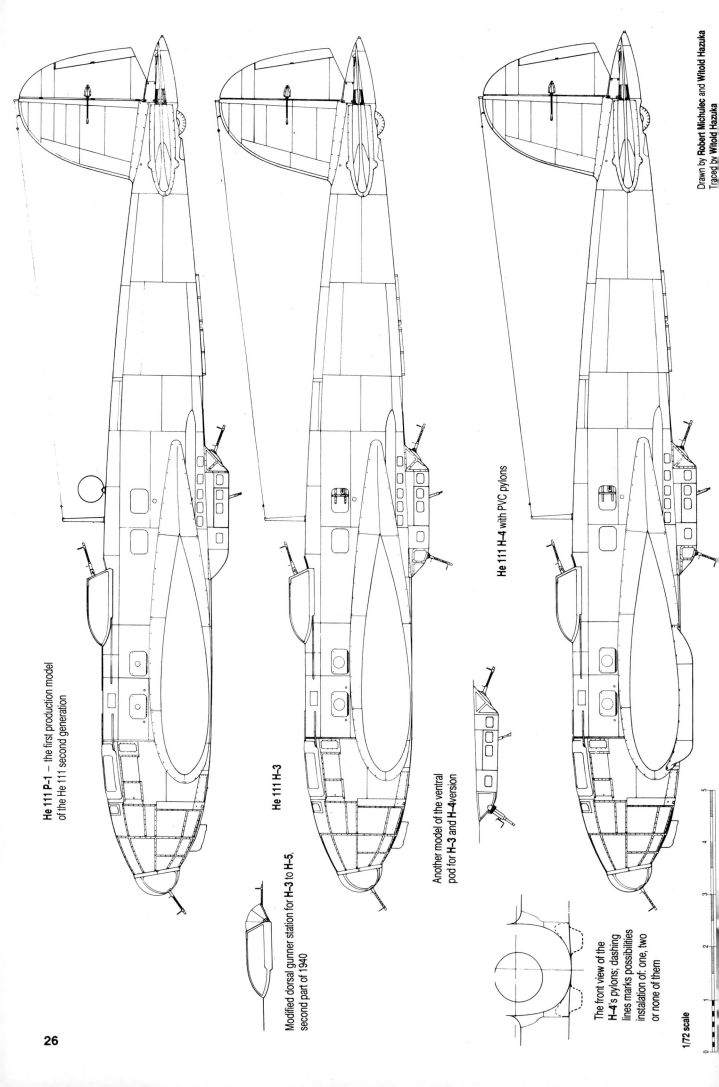

He 111 P-1 – the first production model of the He 111 second generation

He 111 H-3

Modified dorsal gunner station for **H-3** to **H-5**, second part of 1940

Another model of the ventral pod for **H-3** and **H-4** version

He 111 H-4 with PVC pylons

The front view of the **H-4**'s pylons; dashing lines marks possibilities instalation of: one, two or none of them

Drawn by **Robert Michulec** and **Witold Hazuka**
Traced by **Witold Hazuka**

1/72 scale

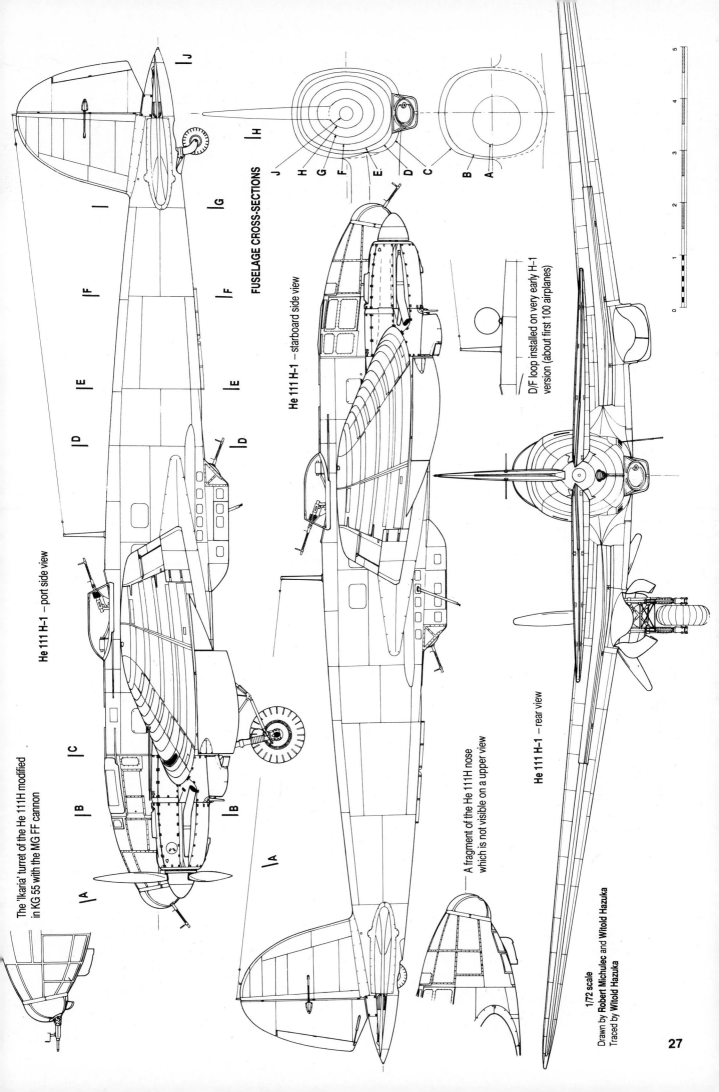

The 'Ikaria' turret of the He 111H modified in KG 55 with the MG FF cannon

He 111 H-1 – port side view

FUSELAGE CROSS-SECTIONS

He 111 H-1 – starboard side view

D/F loop installed on very early H-1 version (about first 100 airplanes)

— A fragment of the He 111H nose which is not visible on a upper view

He 111 H-1 – rear view

1/72 scale

Drawn by **Robert Michulec** and **Witold Hazuka**
Traced by **Witold Hazuka**

27

L

N

M

WING CROSS-SECTIONS

The Junkers wooden
VS 11 propeller used
from H–6

The VDM metal propeller
used to H–5

He 111 H–1 –top view

|M

|L

Top view of the later He 111H
versions cockpit

He 111 H–1 –front view

|L

|M

1/72 scale

Drawn by **Robert Michulec** and **Witold Hazuka**
Traced by **Witold Hazuka**

0   1   2   3   4   5

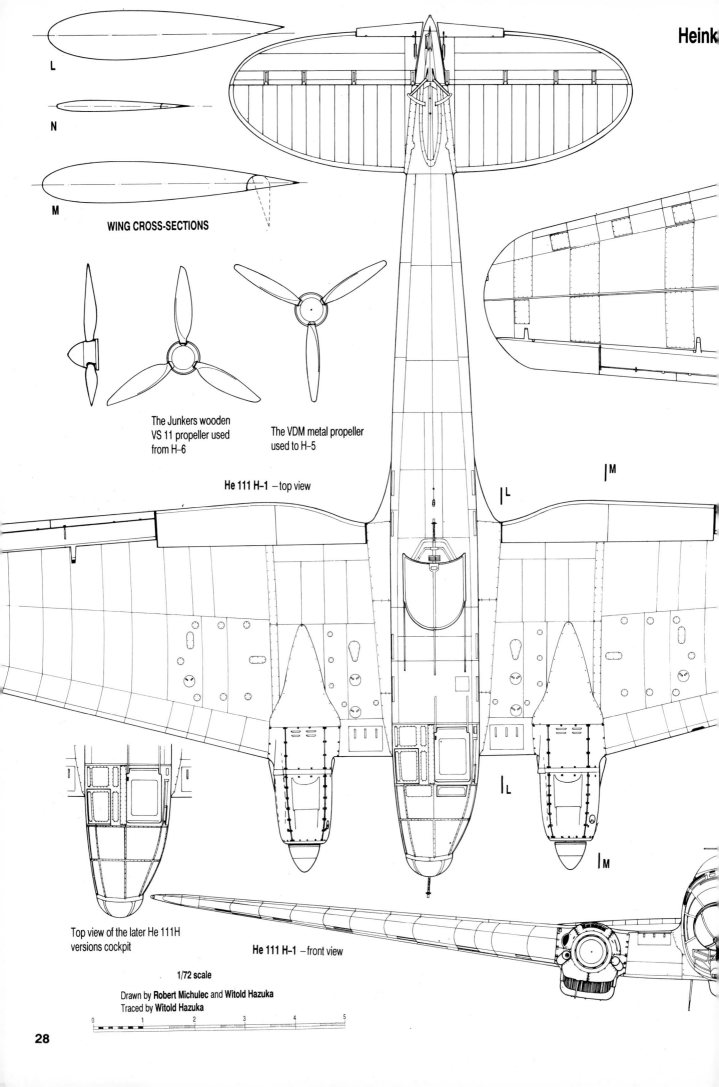

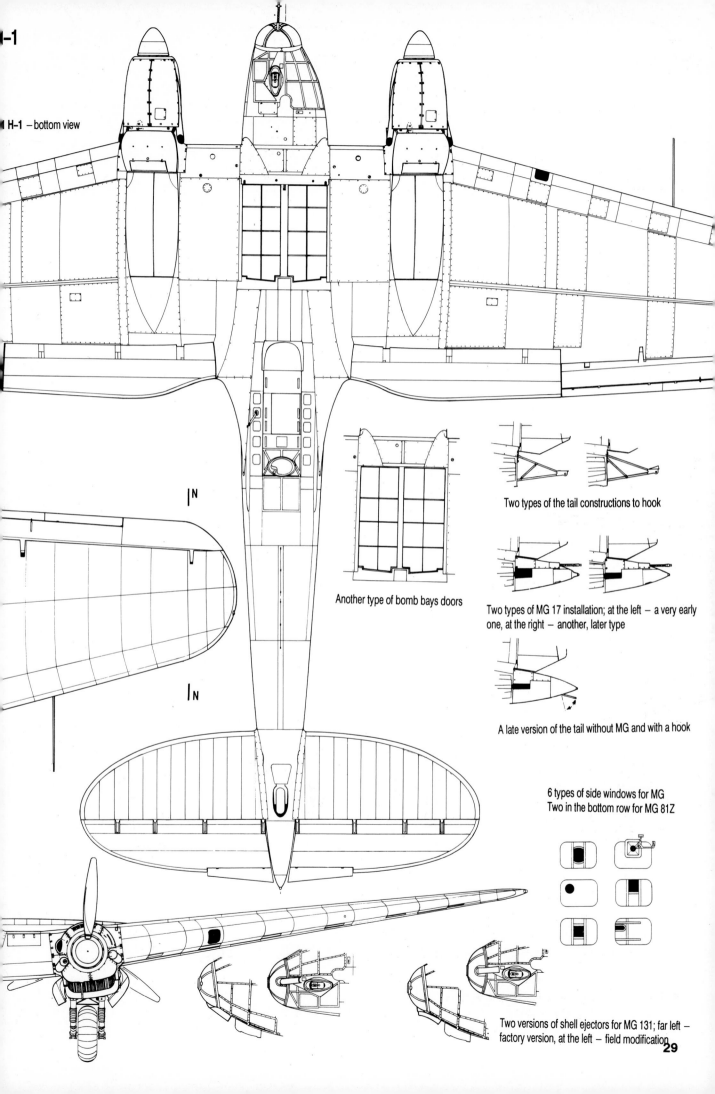

H-1

H-1 – bottom view

Another type of bomb bays doors

Two types of the tail constructions to hook

Two types of MG 17 installation; at the left – a very early one, at the right – another, later type

A late version of the tail without MG and with a hook

6 types of side windows for MG
Two in the bottom row for MG 81Z

Two versions of shell ejectors for MG 131; far left – factory version, at the left – field modification

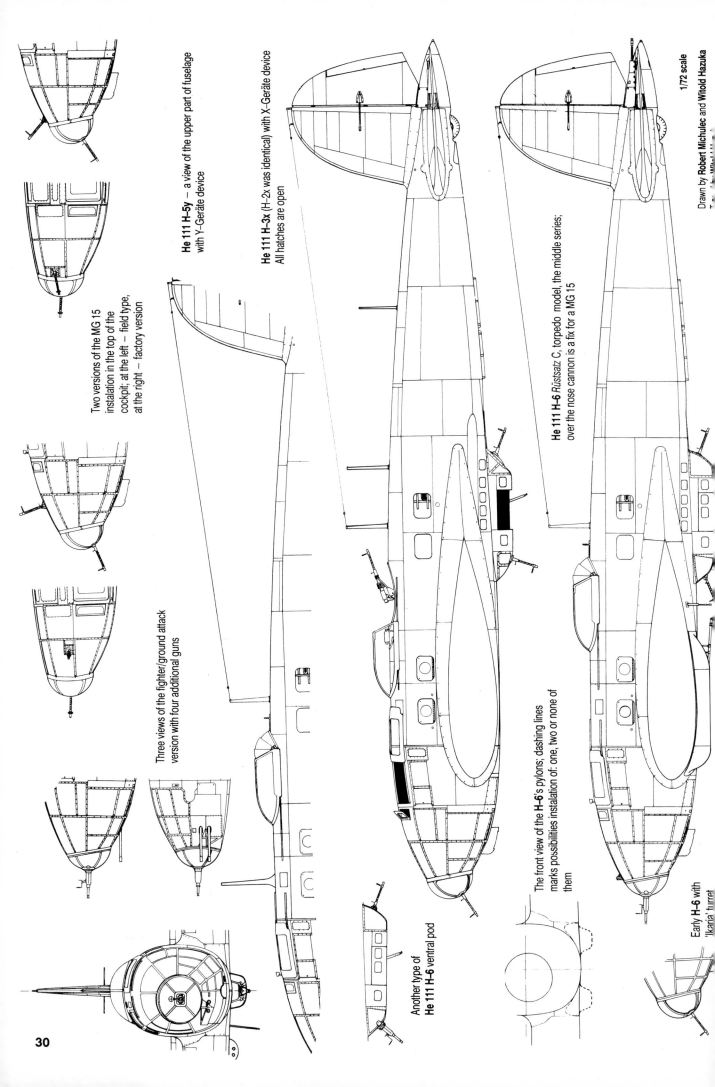

Two versions of the MG 15 instalation in the top of the cockpit; at the left – field type, at the right – factory version

He 111 H-5y – a view of the upper part of fuselage with Y-Geräte device

He 111 H-3x (H-2x was identical) with X-Geräte device All hatches are open

1/72 scale

Drawn by **Robert Michulec** and **Witold Hazuka**

Three views of the fighter/ground attack version with four additional guns

He 111 H-6 *Rüstsatz* C, torpedo model, the middle series; over the nose cannon is a fix for a MG 15

Another type of **He 111 H-6** ventral pod

The front view of the **H-6**'s pylons; dashing lines marks possibilities instalation of: one, two or none of them

Early **H-6** with 'Ikaria' turret

30

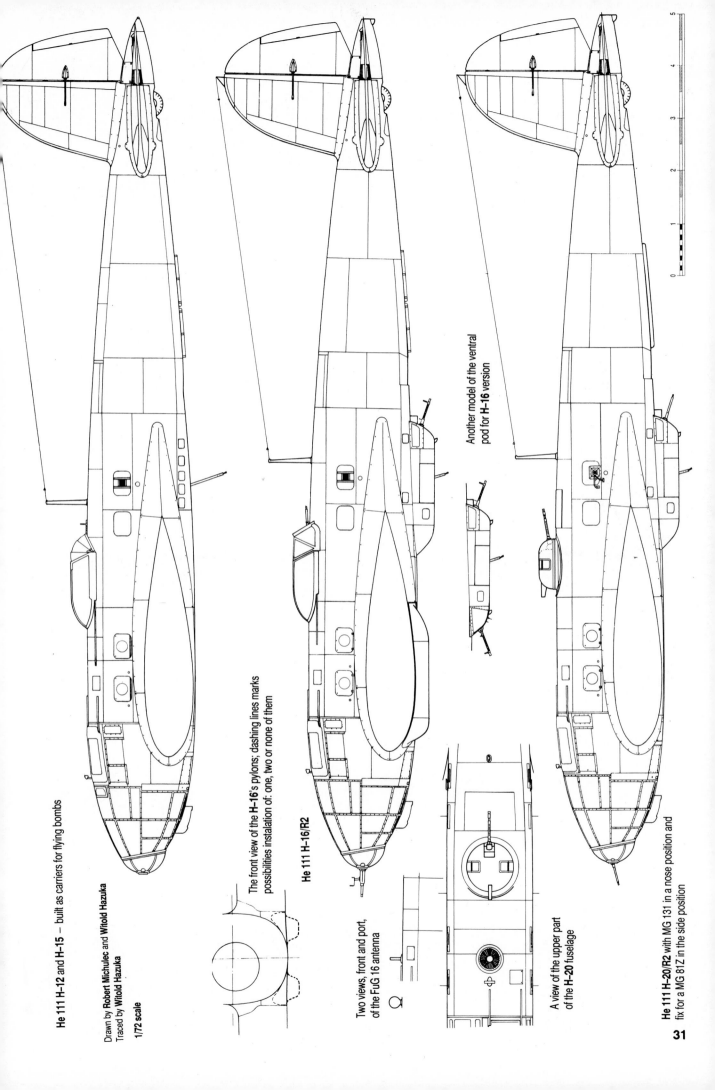

He 111 H-12 and H-15 – built as carriers for flying bombs

Drawn by **Robert Michulec** and **Witold Hazuka**
Traced by **Witold Hazuka**

1/72 scale

The front view of the **H-16**'s pylons; dashing lines marks
possibilities instalation of: one, two or none of them

He 111 H-16/R2

Two views, front and port,
of the FuG 16 antenna

Another model of the ventral
pod for **H-16** version

A view of the upper part
of the **H-20** fuselage

He 111 H-20/R2 with MG 131 in a nose position and
fix for a MG 81Z in the side position

31

The He 111 H-1 with additional armament of III./KG 53 staff flight, northern France, summer 1940. This aircraft is painted in a first version of camouflage with high border – line of upper and lower colours.

Right: The left horizontal fin with Hungarian national colours. This sort of markings were painted at all fins' surfaces.

The end part of right wing of A1 + DA Heinkel with markings of staff aircraft of III./KG 53. These markings were painted only at the top surface of the right wing.

Above: The He 111 P-6 coded F.7+06 of the Hungarian 1/1 Long range recce flight, Kursk, winter 1942/1943. At the vertical fin are a white bars of five aerial victories. The fuselage of aircraft was mainly repainted in RLM 71.

Above: The He 111 H-3x of KGr 100, Northern France, autumn 1940. The crosses at the upper surfaces of wings were small size ones.

Above and below: The He 111 H (export version of H-2) of Groupul 5 bombardment, piloted by commander of one of the Group's flights. Russia, late 1942.

Paint: Sławomir Zajączkowski

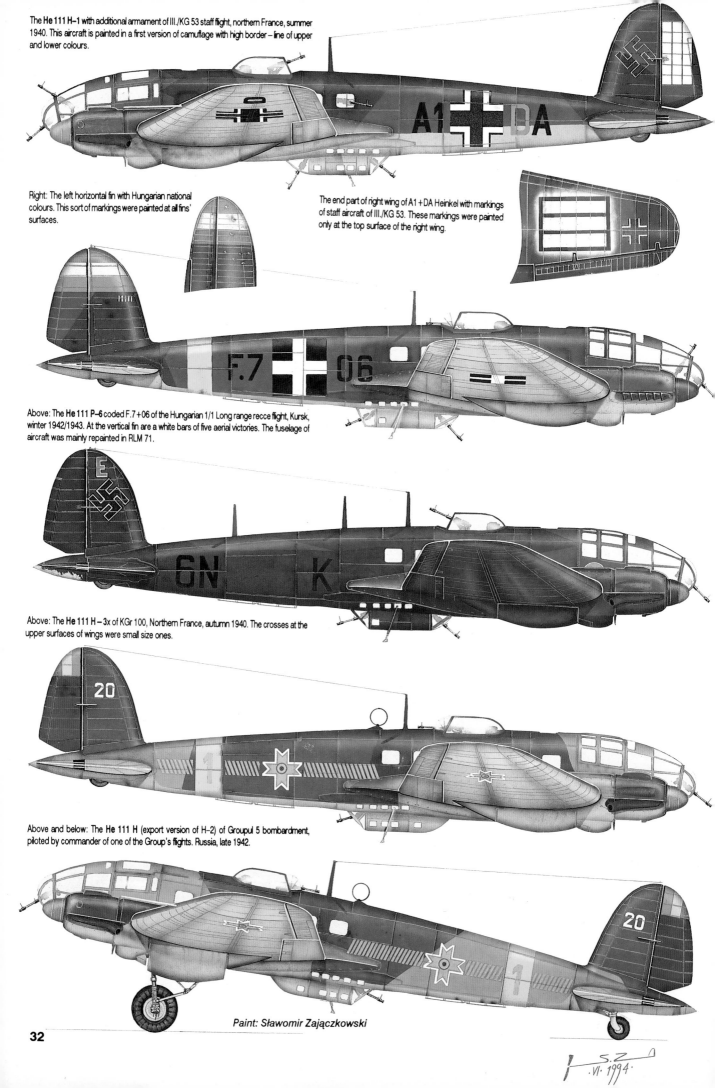

S.Z.
·VI· 1994·

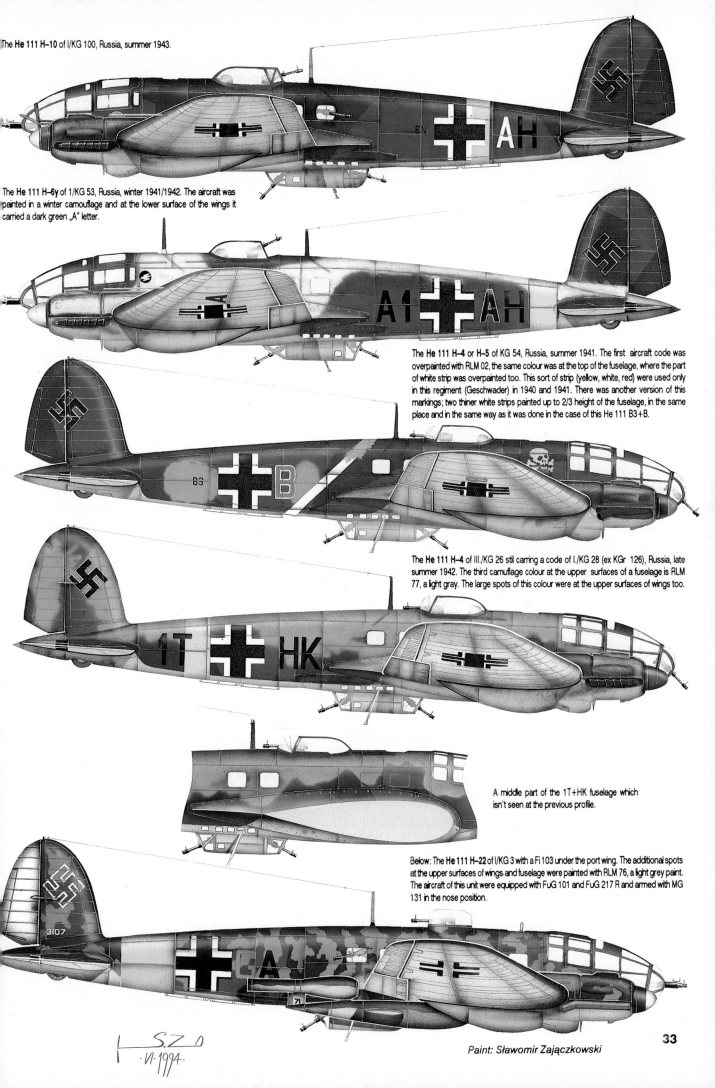

The He 111 H–10 of I/KG 100, Russia, summer 1943.

The He 111 H–6y of 1/KG 53, Russia, winter 1941/1942. The aircraft was painted in a winter camouflage and at the lower surface of the wings it carried a dark green „A" letter.

The He 111 H–4 or H–5 of KG 54, Russia, summer 1941. The first aircraft code was overpainted with RLM 02, the same colour was at the top of the fuselage, where the part of white strip was overpainted too. This sort of strip (yellow, white, red) were used only in this regiment (Geschwader) in 1940 and 1941. There was another version of this markings; two thiner white strips painted up to 2/3 height of the fuselage, in the same place and in the same way as it was done in the case of this He 111 B3+B.

The He 111 H–4 of III./KG 26 stil carring a code of I./KG 28 (ex KGr 126), Russia, late summer 1942. The third camouflage colour at the upper surfaces of a fuselage is RLM 77, a light gray. The large spots of this colour were at the upper surfaces of wings too.

A middle part of the 1T+HK fuselage which isn't seen at the previous profile.

Below: The He 111 H–22 of I/KG 3 with a Fi 103 under the port wing. The additional spots at the upper surfaces of wings and fuselage were painted with RLM 76, a light grey paint. The aircraft of this unit were equipped with FuG 101 and FuG 217 R and armed with MG 131 in the nose position.

33

Paint: Sławomir Zajączkowski

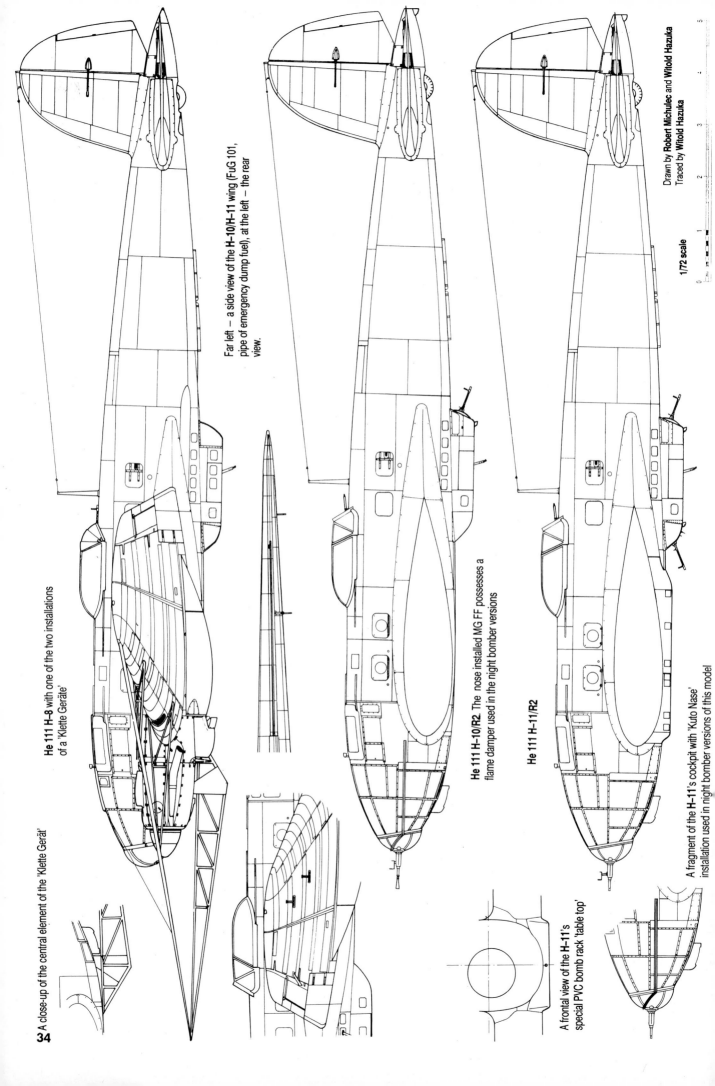

A close-up of the central element of the 'Klette Gerät'

He 111 H-8 with one of the two installations of a 'Klette Gerät'

Far left – a side view of the H-10/H-11 wing (FuG 101, pipe of emergency dump fuel), at the left – the rear view.

He 111 H-10/R2. The nose installed MG FF possesses a flame damper used in the night bomber versions

He 111 H-11/R2

A frontal view of the H-11's special PVC bomb rack 'table top'

A fragment of the H-11's cockpit with 'Kuto Nase' installation used in night bomber versions of this model

Drawn by **Robert Michulec** and **Witold Hazuka**
Traced by **Witold Hazuka**

1/72 scale

34

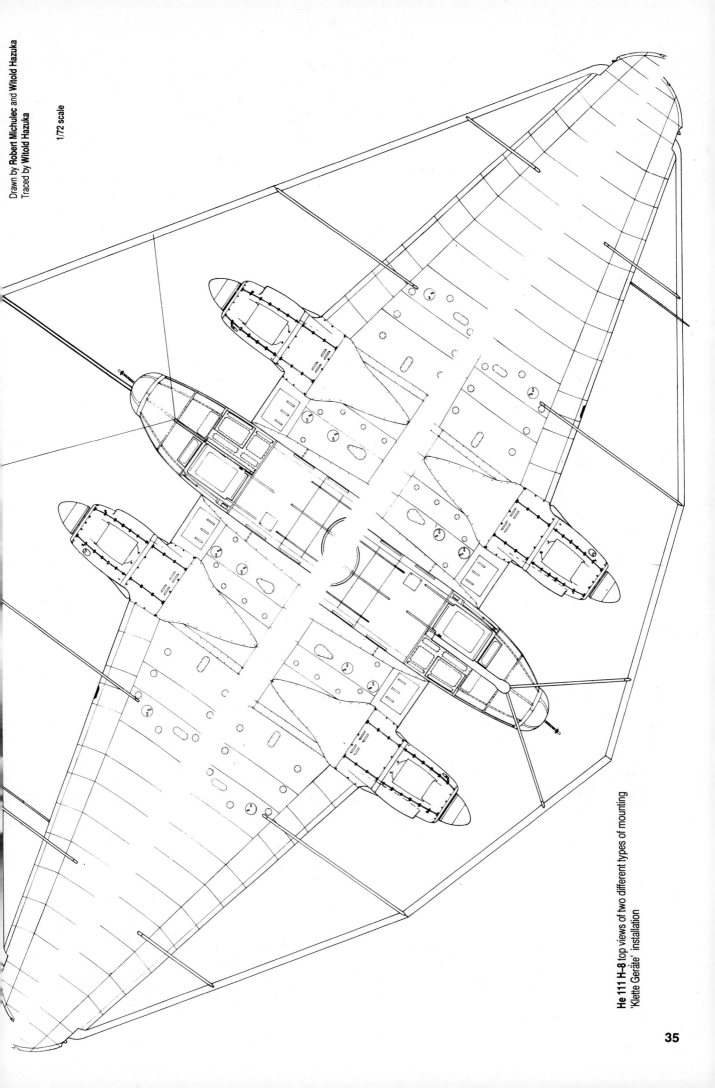

Drawn by **Robert Michulec** and **Witold Hazuka**
Traced by **Witold Hazuka**

1/72 scale

He 111 H-8 top views of two different types of mounting 'Klette Geräte' installation

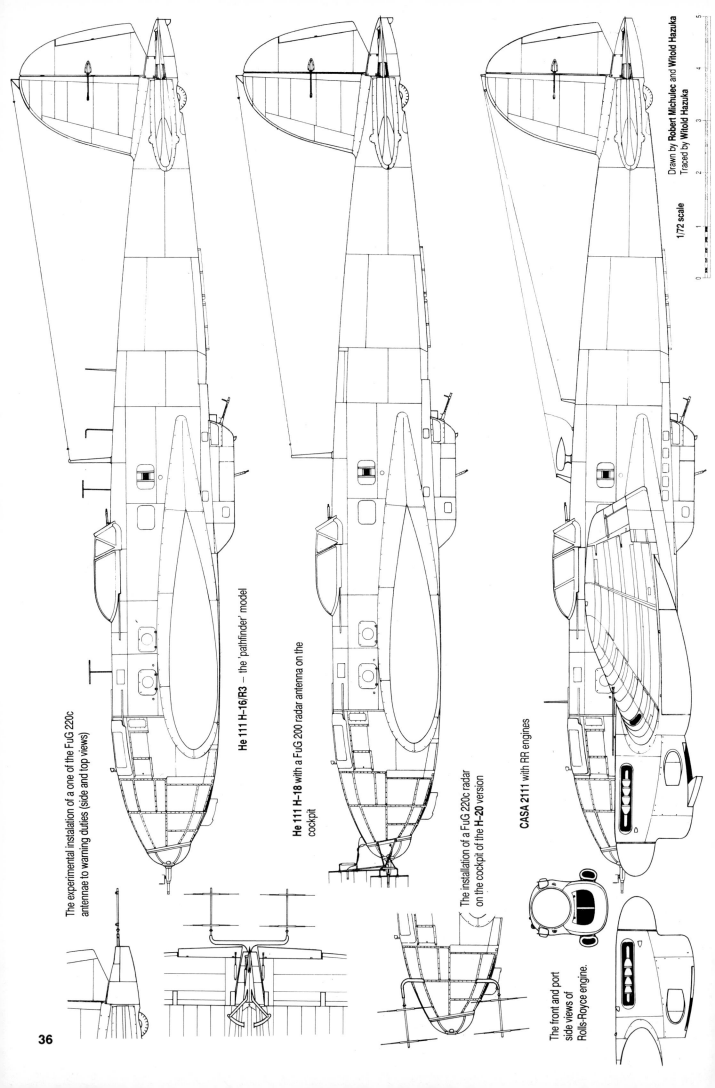

The experimental installation of a one of the FuG 220c antennae to warning duties (side and top views)

He 111 H-16/R3 — the 'pathfinder' model

He 111 H-18 with a FuG 200 radar antenna on the cockpit

The installation of a FuG 220c radar on the cockpit of the **H-20** version

CASA 2111 with RR engines

The front and port side views of Rolls-Royce engine.

Drawn by **Robert Michulec** and **Witold Hazuka**
Traced by **Witold Hazuka**

1/72 scale

36

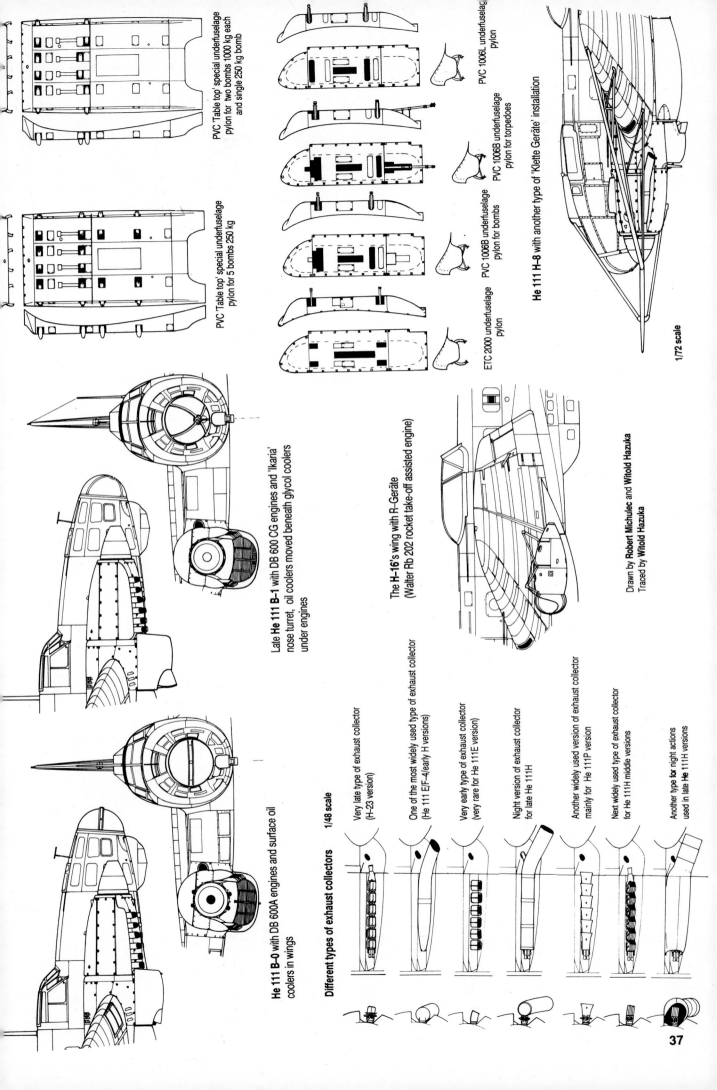

PVC 'Table top' special underfuselage pylon for two bombs 1000 kg each and single 250 kg bomb

PVC 'Table top' special underfuselage pylon for 5 bombs 250 kg

PVC 1006L underfuselage pylon

PVC 1006B underfuselage pylon for torpedoes

PVC 1006B underfuselage pylon for bombs

ETC 2000 underfuselage pylon

He 111 H-8 with another type of 'Klette Geräte' installation

1/72 scale

Late **He 111 B-1** with DB 600 CG engines and 'Ikaria' nose turret, oil coolers moved beneath glycol coolers under engines

The **H-16**'s wing with R-Geräte (Walter Rb 202 rocket take-off assisted engine)

Drawn by **Robert Michulec** and **Witold Hazuka**
Traced by **Witold Hazuka**

He 111 B-0 with DB 600A engines and surface oil coolers in wings

Different types of exhaust collectors   **1/48 scale**

Very late type of exhaust collector (H-23 version)

One of the most widely used type of exhaust collector (He 111 E/F-4/early H versions)

Very early type of exhaust collector (very rare for He 111E version)

Night version of exhaust collector for late He 111H

Another widely used version of exhaust collector mainly for He 111P version

Next widely used type of exhaust collector for He 111H middle versions

Another type for night actions used in late He 111H versions

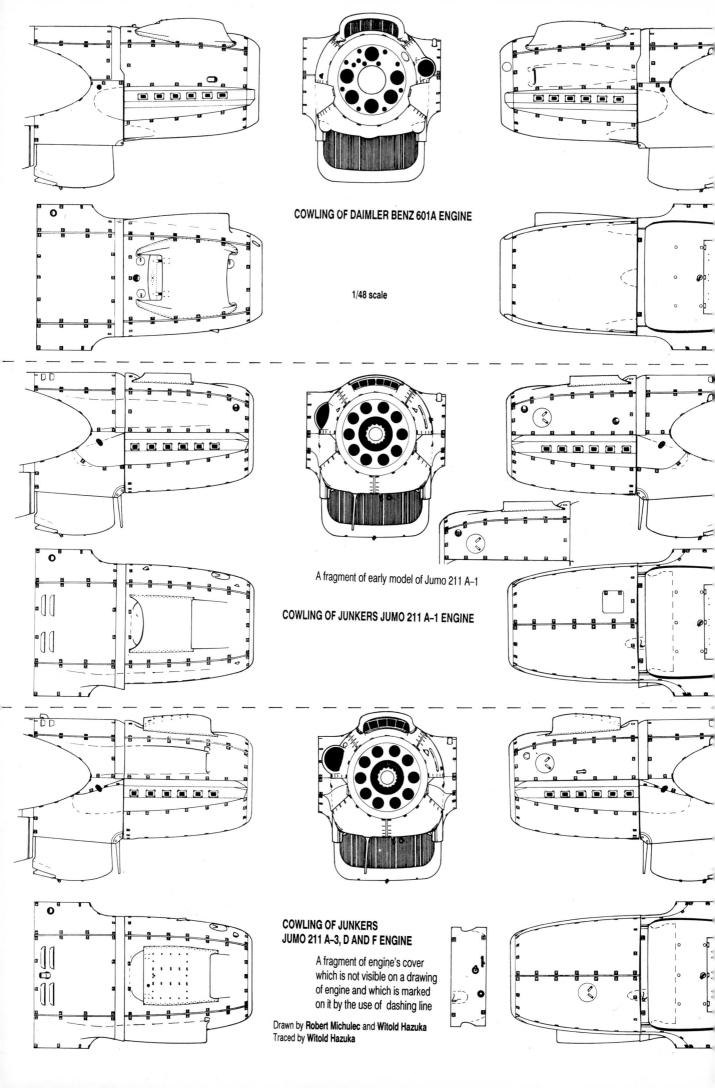

COWLING OF DAIMLER BENZ 601A ENGINE

1/48 scale

A fragment of early model of Jumo 211 A-1

COWLING OF JUNKERS JUMO 211 A-1 ENGINE

**COWLING OF JUNKERS
JUMO 211 A-3, D AND F ENGINE**

A fragment of engine's cover
which is not visible on a drawing
of engine and which is marked
on it by the use of dashing line

Drawn by **Robert Michulec** and **Witold Hazuka**
Traced by **Witold Hazuka**

HEINKEL 111 IN SERVICE

The He 111B–1 coded 25●17 of 1.K/88 with a very dirty (additional painting?) fuselage. The plane have not surface oil coolers.

(IDHYCA via R. Michulec)

OVER SPAIN

The Spanish Civil War, which broke out in August 1936, soon became a pan-European problem, involving directly three other countries. The Republicans received help from the Soviets, while the Nationalists mainly from the Third Reich and Italy. In the agreement between Germany and General Franco, Hitler promised political and military support, an element of this being the 'Condor Legion'. Junkers Ju 52s were the 'Condor Legion's' first bombers, and not until February 1937 did the first four He 111B–1s arrive from Hamburg, accompanied by four Dornier Do 17E–1s and four Junkers Ju 86D–1s. These bombers made up the VBS — Versuchsbomberstaffel (Experimental Bomber Flight) within the K/88 bomber group. One of the basic duties of the crews was to test the aircraft in combat and gather experience in operational use. The He 111 soon gained a reputation as the best among them, and was chosen to equip the staff three aircraft flight of the flight. The section was called 'Pedro' which was painted on each aircraft, and the machine of von Moreau, the VBS K/88 commanding officer, was named 'Pedro 1' and coded 25●3.

During March Heinkel bombers achieved their first success, when attacking the Republican airfield at Alcals de Henares where the K/88 crews claimed the destruction of 24 aircraft and damaging to many others. Next targets for the German crews were on the northern part of the front line, where they flew 2–3, or even 4 mission a day. After a month of activity, on April 26, 1937, General Sperrle gave his crews another task; to make a heavy raid against a road bridge near the small town of Guernica. The bridge was small, old, built at the outskirts of the town, and very important operationally, since through there came the reinforcements for the Republicans in this area. The bomber formation was divided into two groups: the first comprised, among others, two He 111s led by von Moreau, the second 18 Ju 52s led by Fuchs. Both groups arrived on target, dropped their bombs and... destroyed Guernica, leaving the bridge untouched. Many civilian fell victim to the raid, later counted by propagandists at 2500 [1] of which 1645 were killed. The bombing has been considered an example of Nazi terrorist raid policy and became a symbol of Nazi barbarism. This view is still very strong, even though in fact the attack was military justified, and the regrettable destruction of the town followed from errors of the crews and fatal coincidence, partly owing to careless preparation of the raid.

During April (or March), four more He 111 B–1s arrived, and during May the experimental flight started reforming into 1 Staffel K/88. The 2 and 3 Staffeln were re-equipped with Heinkels only in August and September when the equipment started to arrive in large quantities.

The first Heinkel flight was put into action immediately, in the Basque country, which lasted until the end of June. During fighting around Bilbao the K/88 lost its first two Heinkels, but the circumstances are not known. 'Condor Legion' returned to this part of Spain at the end of July, after the Central Front operations ended, but this time the Nationalists encountered stronger opposition in the air, best testified to by the loss of two He 111s in the combat with Esquadrille de Chato 4ᵃ (led by Espes) and Esquadrille de Mosca 3ᵃ (Yevseyev) over the El Musél on August 23. On September 1 the He 111 crews successfully bombed the Republican destroyer Ciscar causing much damage to her. The end of September started a period of bad luck for K/88. On the 30th of that month three He 111s suffered accidents, of which one ended in a write-off, the airframe being later cannibalised for spares. Two subsequent accidents, at the end of October, led to the complete destruction of two more bombers. All these incidents were connected with re-equipping the remaining flights with He 111s. At end October the group had four

flights, of 12 He 111Bs each, and totalled at 52–53 bombers, including 28 He 111 B–2s.

On March 9, during a routine attack against Republican airfields at Caspe (Esquadrille de Mosca 1ᵃ) and Escatrpe (Esquadrille de Mosca 4ᵃ) Heinkels were intercepted by I–16s led by Clavero of 4ᵃ. After a long exchange of fire one was hit and exploded in the air, while another kill claimed by the Republicans cannot be confirmed. The 'Spades' dropped their bombload within airfields, but did not cause any serious damage. On March 27, a group of Heinkels attacked successfully Larida airfield, claiming destruction of four Esquadrille 4ᵃ I–16s. On April 2, this was answered by the Russians who attacked K/88's home base at Alfaro, destroying 2 bombers and damaging 5.

On April 17 the Germans carried out two heavy raids against Cartagena and Almeria, these being the principal Republican ports in this area. The He 111 of 1./K88's CO was lost, while a torpedo boat was sunk, the battleship 'Jaime 1' damaged, and fires started in dockyards. The operation itself seemed fruitful, but the total balance did not. During three days of operation (April 16–18: ferry flight to the area of attack, the attack itself, and the return to the home base) the group lost as many as 8 bombers destroyed (only one to enemy action), and 16 were damaged! As if this was not enough, on April 25,

The He 111B–1 coded 25●22 of 1st Staffel of K/88, Spain 1937. Note untypical shape of numbers.

(IDHYCA via R. Michulec)

The He 111B–1 named „Pedro 6", Spain, early summer 1937. The some aircraft was painted on upper surfaces with RLM 63 and large spots of RLM 64.

(IDHYCA via R. Michulec)

Esquadrille 3a I–16s shot down three more at Valencia.

On May 25, 1938 the Republicans started the Ebro river offensive. K/88 was responsible for almost the whole air support of the Nationalists, this being extremely difficult as the reinforcements in the form of 25 He 111E–1s started to come only at the beginning of July and continued until September. The next 10 aircraft arrived at the beginning of January 1939, this being the last delivery for the 'Condor Legion'.

The Battle of Ebro lasted until November 1938 and involved extensive use of air power, which led to heavy and bloody air battles. Two He 111 – equipped units took part in these; the German K/88 and Spanish 10–G–25. Losses were high on both sides, luckily not affecting K/88 too much. The only He 111 lost to enemy action during that period was shot down by Arias' Esquadrille 4ª. During just one air battle over Reus, Arias' fighters and those from Pereira's Esquadrille 5ª claimed the destruction of 4 He 111s and setting another on fire. Even though these data might seem exaggerated, it is a fact that on December 23, both units had in all only 30 serviceable He 111s, 25 of these in K/88. This means that out of 24 'Spades' of the Spanish unit, 19 had been lost, destroyed or damaged. The Germans lost 2 He 111s during that time, and 8 more were damaged. Combined attacks and demonstration flight over Madrid in the Spring 1939 were the last activity of the K/88.

These consisted in formation flying of up to 30 He 111s with no opposition from the enemy, and dropping individual bombs on various targets. Ironically, during one such flight on March 12, the bombload exploded on board the machine of Major Harle, the K/88 CO, killing all the crew. 15 days later the 'Condor Legion' He 111s carried out their last mission under the Iberian sky, and next 19 days later the three-years long civil war was ended. The German 'Legion' returned home, leaving the aircraft behind. Out of 33 He 111 B–1s, 28 B–2s and 35 E–1s (the highest known B–1 code is 25●32, the lowest known B–2 code is 25●34, the highest He 111 code of all is 25●96) sent to Spain, 37 were lost during 1937 – 39, of which 20 were lost to enemy action (listed in the Table 1). 'Condor Legion' B–1s can be distinguished most easily from the B–2s by the camouflage used on these machines. Apart from the first six-eight B–1s, of which the first four were from the early B–1 series with DB 600A engines, all the rest were painted RLM 02 or RLM 63 overall, while the B–2s and E–1/E–3s (and of course the first 6 – 8 B–1s) were in the RLM 61/62/63/65 camouflage. It is not impossible that some more He 111 reached Spain (see EXPORTS – Spain).

THE SUCCESS OF THE DOUHET THEORY

By all the evidence Hitler won his first battle in 1938 thanks to the Luftwaffe bombers which made a deep impression on West European politicians, given them another reason to give Hitler a part of Czechoslovakia.

The successful Anschluss of Austria led Hitler in September 1938 to another milestone in his European policy, the Czech Sudetenland question which provoked the Munich crisis. At that time, in spite of being one of the most powerful countries in Europe, the Third Reich was on the edge of an economic crisis and completely unprepared for war, so it could not have fought for more than a few weeks. However, the war did not start thanks to the appeasement policy of the West European authorities, and to the successful blackmail value of the Luftwaffe, especially the bombers. According to the Western powers, no great European capital city could withstand their strike, to say nothing about 'a Prague'. During the Munich crisis German aviation possessed 3200 combat aircraft, including 1235 bombers. 570 He 111s formed the backbone of the force, equipping eight Geschwadern: KG 152, 154, 155, 157, 253, 254, 257 and 355, of which KG 154 'Boelcke' (ex-KG 157) was the oldest user, since the winter 1936. This was not, however, a winning force, since France had 3650 aircraft at that time, Britain 3300 aircraft, and Czechoslovakia 1500. Of these 4050 allied machines were in front line units, including 1850 bombers. It is a fact that these aircraft were mostly obsolete and could not equal German types, but in terms of numbers they were supreme. In spite of that, the French and British politicians succumbed to the experience of the Spanish war and to the warnings of their experts. Sholto Douglas, an RAF staff officer, felt increasing fear of the German Heinkels, while Gen. Vuillemin, the CO of the French Armee de l'Air assured his Prime Minister that the French aviation would cease to exist after a few days of war. They were both, however, surpassed by Col. Charles Lindbergh [3] who would overwhelm them with arguments about the power of the Luftwaffe, capable not only of destroying the French and British air forces, but also of turning the capitals of these countries into rubble and destroying their independence.

The blackmailed ministers, threatened by the vision of He 111s destroying London or Paris, successfully suggested that their superiors give Czechoslovakia to Hitler, thus giving them another argument for that decision. Hitler, on his part, had every reason to thank Ernst Heinkel, and above all the Günter brothers, since it is no exaggeration that their bomber [4] largely contributed to winning this political battle.

OVER POLAND

In the Spring 1939 Germany's firs line air force employed 3368 combat machines in the front line, mostly modern types. According to the German doctrine which favoured attack and maximum destruction to the enemy, bombers were more numerous in the Luftwaffe.

On September 1, there was 1,180 of these, including 808 He 111s, of which 749 were P and H versions.

They equipped the following units:
●Stab, II, III(K)/LG 1 — 99 He 111H — Poland
●Stab, I, II/KG 1 — 82 He 111H, E, F — Poland
●Stab, I, II, III/KG 4 — 102 He 111P — Poland
●Stab, I, II/KG 26 — 75 He 111H (only Stab and II Gruppe used over Poland)
●Stab, I, II, III/KG 27 — 94 He 111P — Poland II/KG 28 — 35 He 111H
●Stab, I, III/KG 51 — 78 He 111H
●Stab, I, II, III/KG 53 — 105 He 111H — (only I Gruppe used over Poland)
●Stab, I/KG 54 — 45 He 111H — (only 2 flights over Poland from 3.09.1939
●Stab, I, II, III/KG 55 — 73 He 111H — (only I and II Gruppen over Poland from 3.09.1939
●1 Wekusta/Ob.d.L. — 8 He 111J
●Wekusta 51 — 6 He 111J
●Wekusta 1 — 3 He 111J
●Wekusta 76 — 3 He 111J
●2(F)/122 — 11 He 111H
●10(M)/LG 2 — 9 He 111
●Ln.Abt. 100 — 9 He 111H

Table 1

A He 111 losses of K/88 *Legion Condor* in Spain [2]

Quantity, Type	Area	Date	Notes
2 He 111B	Bilbao	05.1937	one lost in accident
2 He 111B	Santander	23.08.	shot-down by fighters
1 He 111B	Gijón	02.09.	shot-down by fighters
1 He 111B	Albericia	30.09.	crashed
1 He 111B	Albericia	21.10.	accidents
1 He 111B	Albericia	24.10.	
1 He 111B	Candasnos	10.12.	shot-down by fighters
1 He 111B	Sierra de Guadalajara	17.12.	captured by Republicians
1 He 111B	Teruél	26.01.1938	shot-down by AA fire or by fighters
1 He 111B	Bujaraloz	11.03.	shot-down by fighters
2 He 111B	Alfaro	02.04.	destroyed in sortie
1 He 111B	Fraga	the end 03.	shot-down by fighters
1 He 111B	Cabaza de Vace	16.04.	crashed in mountains
6 He 111B	Granada	16–17.04.	lost in bed weather
1 He 111B	near Motril	17.04.	shot-down by AA fire
3 He 111B	near Valencia	25.04.	shot-down by fighters
1 He 111B	?	14.05.	shot-down by AA fire or by fighters
1 He 111B	?	29.05.	shot-down by AA fire or by fighters
1He 111E	near Barcelona	31.10.	shot-down by fighters
1 He 111E or B	Pinell	02.11.	shot-down by Nationalists AA fire
1 He 111E or B	Tarragona	04.01.1939	shot-down by AA fire or by fighters
1 He 111E or B	Ocejo	17.01.	shot-down by AA fire or by fighters
1 He 111E or B	Arreus	25.01.	crashed in mountains

Moreover, approximately 20–30 He 111s were used for courier duties during the war with Poland and in Germany, and in all the Germans possessed about 850 He 111s in the versions E (38 aircraft in I/KG 1), H, J, P.

Warsaw was the area of most He 111 activity. On the first day of the war the Germans carried out two raids against airfields around the city. The first, in the morning, which involved 30 bombers of II(K)/LG 1 escorted by Bf 110s of I(Z)/LG 1, came to nothing because of the resistance of the Brygada Pościgowa (the Pursuit Brigade, the fighter unit responsible for the air defence of Warsaw) and bad weather. The second raid, on the other hand, carried out by 60 bombers of KG 27 escorted by 30 fighters, brought the decimation of the Polish fighters in air combat, and numerous hits at the three airfields attacked; Mokotów, Okęcie and Gocław. Subsequent raids were carried out on September 2, and then they gradually ceased until September 16, when 12 He 111s of I/KG 4 attacked Warsaw directly, not just a military target within the city limits. Next, air attacks were made on September 18, 19 and 22, and on 24 and 25 a two-day bombing campaign against the Polish capital was carried out by 400 bombers.

On September 25 alone the Germans flew 1776 sorties, dropping 500 tonnes of iron bombs and 72 tonnes of incendiary bombs. A large part of the city lay in rubble, including many historical buildings, and three days later Warsaw surrendered. Thus, thanks to two heavy air raids the Germans crushed resistance and avoided heavy losses of the ground forces. The bombers had proved effective again.

On September 1, some 60 He 111s of I and III/KG 4 carried out a heavy attack against Cracow airfield, while II/KG 4 went to Lwów (now Lvov, Ukraine) where they lost a single plane. The Rakowice airfield at Cracow was destroyed by 48 tonnes of bombs, and the Skniepy airfield at Lwów by 22 tonnes. Similar tasks were performed on the next day, when a heavy blow by 88 Heinkels inflicted much destruction on the three airfields of the Dęblin area, where 11 aircraft were also destroyed. During the whole Battle of Poland, KG 4 'General Wever' lost a total of 5 bombers including 2 He 111s in one combat on September 6. In the area of Grójec 3./KG 4 Heinkels successfully bombed the motorised echelon of the Polish III/6 dyon (squadron), but a moment later the section of Oberlt. Kell was attacked by a group of PZL P.11s, led by ppor. (2nd Lt) Główczyński of the same squadron. During the combat 2 He 111s were shot down, and a third, that of Kell's, was damaged with 70 rounds without loss to Polish fighters. 7 men died, 3 were wounded.

In the following days communication lines, mainly railways (and especially the overcrowded stations) were the principal targets for the German bombers. The crowded roads, full of evacuated civilians and dispersed military units, were also attacked. Formations of bombers used the Polish sky without problems, often even in small groups without fighter cover. The maximum speed of the He 111H and P was about 400 km/h, i.e. more than that of Polish fighters, which allowed escape provided the fighters were spotted early. During the whole campaign Polish fighters claimed 83 bombers, while the anti-aircraft artillery claimed three times as many. Among the bombers claimed by Polish fighters, 41 were He 111s, while the AAA identified 10 of their prey as He 111s. In fact the Germans lost 78 bombers over Poland.

OVER THE NORTH SEA

After the Battle of Poland effectively ended, on September 22, the Germans started to transfer their units to the West. Even though France was their principal enemy, until May 1940 the

The He 111B–2 coded 25●26 of 2.K/88, Spain 1938. Note exhaust pipes of old style.

(R. Michulec coll.)

main targets were outside the continental, on the North Sea and in Britain. The brunt of the war was carried by KG 26 'Löwen' (Lions) and this unit claimed the most successes during the 'Phoney war', and also most losses. It started with losses, and heavy ones.

On October 9, 1939, a German reconnaissance aircraft discovered a group of ships consisting of 3 cruisers and 2 destroyers near Egersund. 148 bombers scrambled, including 127 He 111s of Stab, I, II/KG 26 and II, III(K)/LG 1, but only some 10 aircraft reached the target! What is more, no hits were obtained, and 4 He 111s were lost in accidents on their way back! Another He 111 was written off KG 26's inventory on October 28, 1939, when Lt. R. Niehoff of Stab/KG 26 was caught and shot up by 6 *Spitfires* of 602 and 603 Squadrons, RAF. The aircraft force-landed in Britain and was the first machine shot down over British soil. A similar fate befell a 5./KG 26 He 111 flown by Unteroffizier H. Mayer on February 9, 1940. It was damaged by *Spitfires* of 602 Squadron but this time the landing was much finer and the Heinkel was later repaired and used by the RAF. However, attempts to capture German bombers intact were not always successful. On February 22, 1940, two 602 Squadron pilots intercepted an He 111, this time a P variant of (F) Ob.d.L. After a short pursuit and a lot of shooting the 'Spade' was damaged and forced to land. One of the British pilots, Farquhar, decided to land beside the Heinkel so as to prevent the crew from destroying their machine. Unfortunately for the British pilot, during the landing his *Spitfire* turned over and trapped him in the cockpit, whereupon the German crew, led by Lt. Grote set their aircraft on fire and only then released their tormentor.

January 1940 was full of serious combat for KG 26. During four days (9–12 January), the Geschwader sank 7 ships for the loss of 2 He 111s shot down, including one from AA fire, and another damaged. Still greater success was achieved on January 30, when 26 crews of I and II/KG 26 sank four ships for only one Heinkel lost and one damaged. On February 2, 24 He 111s of I and II Gruppen were intercepted by *Hurricanes* of 43 Squadron and *Hudsons* of 46 Squadron, and during two hours of protracted pursuit and fighting 3 were shot down and 3 more damaged, while the Germans shot down a *Hudson* and sank one ship.

February 22 was a terrible day for the Germans. During the first of two operations by KG 26 on that day, an He 111 was damaged by AA fire during a fruitless attack against a group of ships laying mines, while during the second Feldwebel Jager of 4/KG 26 used two series of bombs to direct the German destroyer 'Leberecht Maass' into a minefield where she was sunk. On the same night Kriegsmarine gunners gained revenge, in a sense, by shooting down a He 111 of KGr 100, this being the first day of combat operations for the unit.

During March I/KG 26 successfully attacked a major group of ships only once, on March 20 when they damaged five of these and sank another shortly after. During these actions 2 He 111s were shot down by a *Hurricane* of 43 Squadron RAF and a *Skua* of 803 Squadron, Fleet Air Arm.

Combat activity of the bomber units over France was almost non-existent, only the 'leaflet war' was carried out over the Maginot Line. This does not, however mean that there were no losses. For example, on November 17, 1939, several

The same aircraft as above. The 'Ikaria' turret is very well visible.

(R Michulec coll.)

The He 111H–6y of KG53 'Legion Condor' Geschwader, Russia, winter 1941/42.

crews of I and II/KG 51 left on such sorties, two of which never returned because of the terrible weather. Of the 8 men only one survived.

The last He 111 lost during the 'Phoney war' was an aircraft of the Stab/KG 1 flown by Lt. Lehmann, shot down in combat with 5 MS 406s of GC II/3 at Maastricht.

OVER NORWAY

The actions preceding the Allied landing in Norway started on April 9, 1940, and involved X Fliegerkorps which included the following Heinkel units:
- Stab, I,II, III/KG 4 — 95 He 111P
- Stab, I, II, III/KG 26 — 103 He 111H
- KGr 100 — 27 He 111H
- 1(F)/120 — 3 He 111H (+5 Dornier Do 17P)
- 1(F)/122 — 8 He 111H
- Others — 6 He 111H

These units accounted for 242 Heinkel 111s of a total of 396 bombers. It is interesting to note that the X Fliegerkorps had 1086 aircraft in all, of which 282 were transports and only 98 fighters! This gives a bomber to fighter ration of about 4:1, a proportion rather out of standard for other campaigns. What is also interesting is that the German forces were later reinforced by further bomber units, including two using He 111s: I, II/KG 54 and II, III/LG 1. Operation 'Weserübung' was also supported by some other units destined to operate over the routes of British convoys and along British coasts, that were not subject to X Fliegerkorps. One of these was KüFlGr FlGrFlGr806, a unit which could not claim any successes, while meeting several failures. When protecting their own fleet they did not prevent the Polish submarine 'Orzel' from sinking the transport ship 'Rio de Janeiro' with 97 men of 33 AAA regiment on board; and on May 11–12 they carried out unsuccessful

attacks against the British RZ force, losing an He 111J shot down and another damaged.

The whole 'Weserübung' operation was essentially carried out in two parts, but the outcome of the battle was decided in the first two days. On April 9 the Luftwaffe made eight major raids in which coastal artillery batteries, naval bases and airfields were attacked. The two strongest groups of the He 111s were sent to the capitals of Norway and Denmark to ... drop leaflets. The principal event on that day took place to the west of Norway, on the North Sea, where a large sea-air battle was fought between 28 British ships and 88 German aircraft, including 41 He 111s of KG 26. It resulted in the loss of 4 Junkers Ju 88s and a destroyer, while 4 cruisers were damaged. Additionally the Norwegian destroyer 'čeger' was sunk at Stavanger by a single He 111 of KG 4. The next day X Fliegerkorps reinforcements continued similar operations with similar results, but this time more He 111s were shot down and 3 damaged (the previous day only 3 He 111s were lost, including one damaged). It is worth noting the disabling of a Norwegian radio station by an He 111 of III(K)/LG 1 which struck the mast with a wing, and the destruction of three aircraft on two airfields by another He 111 of the same unit.

Despite conquering Norway in a few days, a dangerous enemy remained in the form of the British fleet and an Allied expeditionary corps. The British maintained strong resistance in the north of the country until June of that year and inflicted serious losses on the Germans. Contrary to April when no important Allied ships were accounted for, during May the Germans achieved some notable strikes. On May 2 a sadist crew of II/LG 1 bombed at Namsos the clearly marked Norwegian hospital ship 'Dronning

Maud', killing many on board and rendering the ship useless, and later attacked Gratangen village, destroying several houses and killing two civilians. On May 4 a group of 13 He 111s of KGr 100 found the Polish destroyer 'Grom' and sank her in three minutes with a single precise salvo of bombs. The same fate overtook the Polish merchant ship 'Chrobry', sunk by 6 He 111s of I/KG 26 on May 15, and the cruiser, HMS 'Curlew', sunk by KGr 100 on May 26. The latter loss was particularly significant for the Allies since the cruiser carried a radar station for observation of the Norwegian air space.

The second phase of the Norwegian campaign also brought numerous air combats. The greatest air battle of this campaign was fought on April 25 near Lake Lejaskog where the British airfield was situated. On the morning of that day a single He 111 destroyed four *Gladiators* of 263 Squadron, and a little later 19 Heinkels of II(K)/LG 1 carried out a heavy attack destroying another 10 British aircraft. This was not the end however, for individual attacks were made throughout the day, and in total 19 British machines were lost for the price of 5 German bombers, including 4 He 111s. On May 14, at Vaernes near Trondheim, during a combat between 803 Squadron FAA and II/KG 26, Lt. W.P. Lucy, the best Royal Navy *Skua* pilot, and victor over the German cruiser 'Konigsberg', was killed by return fire from the German gunners. On May 22, at Salangen in another combat, M. A. Craig — Adams of 263 Squadron rammed an He 111 of II/KG 26 with his *Gladiator*. A week later, on May 29, a combat over Narvik between 9 *Hurricanes* of 46 Squadron and 11 He 111s of KGr 100 resulted in the commander of the latter unit, Hptm. von Casimir, being shot down, after the bomber's gunners claimed one fighter shot down by themselves and another shared. In total the Luftwaffe lost 61 He 111s over Norway (including 7 non-combat losses) and 31 damaged. 42 Heinkels were shot down in air combat, while their gunners claimed 10 enemy aircraft. 21 Allied aircraft were destroyed on the ground by bombs, and no less than 15 ships were sunk.

OVER FRANCE

The period of tension in the still-free part of Europe following the conquest of Poland lasted for six months, and the Germans used it to carefully prepare for the operation against Hitler's principal antipathy — France. The Luftwaffe grew by 1000 aircraft after September 1939, including 600 bombers, yet it was still inferior to the Allies in terms of numbers.

In early May 1940 it possessed 1758 bombers, including 850 He 111s, allocated to the following main bomber units:
- II(K)/LG 1 — 36 He 111
- Stab, I, II, III/KG 4 — 67 He 111
- Stab, III/KG 51 — 42 He 111
- Stab, I, II, III/KG 1 — 98 He 111
- Stab, I, II, III/KG 26 99 He 111
- Stab, I, II, III/KG 27 — 106 He 111
- Stab, I, II, III/KG 53 — 112 He 111
- Stab, I, II, III/KG 54 — 110 He 111 Stab, I, II, III/KG 55 — 108 He 111
- KGr 100 — 27 He 111
- KGr 126 — 32 He 111

For the war against France, the Germans allocated Luftflotten 2 and 3, which possessed 1120 bombers in total, including 675 He 111s in service with the above units, with the exception of those operating over Norway (KG 26, KGr 100 and part of LG 1).

The attack was launched early on the morning of May 10, 1940, with a mass air strike against

The He 111H–4 or H–5 of the KG26 during refuelling with Italian petrol at Sicily or Libya. On the underfuselage bomb racks are two auxiliary fuel tanks 600 litres capacity each.

(R. Michulec coll.)

The He 111H–3x of KGr 100 after force landing.

Allied airfields which destroyed large numbers of aircraft. The Belgians suffered the heaviest losses, as the attacks (by amongst others KG 51 and 53) destroyed 28 fighters, including 9 Hurricanes, and by the end of the next evening the wrecks of some 80 combat aircraft lay on the airfields.

In all, the first day of the invasion brought the destruction of some 200 aircraft by the German bombers for the loss of 77 of their number, including 44 'Spades'. The heaviest losses were sustained by KG 1, 4, and 55, where whole squadrons of 8–9 aircraft were annihilated. A true slaughter of Heinkels of III/KG 54 was made by Fokker D.XXIs of JaVa 1 of the Dutch Luchtmacht, which intercepted the unit over Den Helder, attacking the front and middle of the formation and shot down 7 He 111s one by one, including 6 aircraft of the 8 Staffel. Similar attacks were carried out for two more days but with less success because of the dispersion of Allied aircraft. A similar operation under the — haw atractive — code name 'Paula' was carried out at the beginning of June at the beginning of the second phase of the Battle of France. Just as on May 10, June 3 saw large groups of Luftwaffe bombers attack French airfields around Paris, inflicting heavy losses and disabling the French air force which lacked logistics support. The most important events took place in Flanders which had witnessed the tragedy at Dunkirk a few days earlier. The Allied forces encircled since May 26, were subject to heavy air strikes, of which the first, carried out on May 27, by the He 111s of KG 1, 4, and 54, was one of the heaviest. The bombs struck beaches, port and dockyards, where the vessel 'Aden' was destroyed. During the whole operation more than 250 Allied evacuation vessels fell victim to them.

During the war in Western Europe, Heinkels took part in two dramatic events. The first was the bombing on May 10 of the German city of Freiburg by a crew from KG 51, which caused the deaths of 57 people, including many children. The German authorities were unaware of the fact at first since the crew reported attacking a French city, but after investigation the error was discovered. Needless to say, the case was exploited by the German propaganda and only revealed to the Allies after the war. The other incident was the bombing of Rotterdam in circumstances which are still controversial.

The first raid against Ypenburg airfield near Rotterdam was carried out by 30 He 111s of I/KG 4, causing the whole of JaVa 2 to be grounded. Rear gunner Feldwebel Bruckner shot down one of the few Fokker D.XXIs that managed to take off. I Gruppe suffered no losses during the attack. At the same time other elements of KG 4, namely Stab and II Gruppe, carried out a raid against Walhaven airfield, where 12 Fokker G–Is of JaVa 3 were based, but in this case no serious damage occurred. Two G–Is, flown by Lts. Sonderman and Nomen, took off to intercept the Germans. The former shot down the He 111 of Oberst Fiebig, the Geschwader CO, while the latter shot down two other machines while being damaged himself, and a further two He 111s were claimed by the Dutch AA fire. Soon afterwards, the same airfields were subject to attack by III/KG 4, but this was also intercepted by a lone Fokker G–I flown by Lt. Knipers of JaVa 3 and 2–3 Fokker D.XXIs of JaVa 5. After a long fight in which his own machine was damaged, Knipers claimed two He 111s shot down and another damaged, when in fact he shot down 3 Junkers Ju 88s of the same unit. The JaVa 5 pilot claimed one He 111, while they actually downed two.

Engines replacement in the one of KG4 He 111 planes with help of captured RAF crane. (This is probably a He 111P version). *(R. Michulec coll.)*

Shortly after the Heinkels Junkers Ju 52s arrived over Ypenburg and dropped the 3rd battalion of Fallschrimjager Regt I which was to capture the airfield and hold it for the rest of the day, when subunits from 9 Panzer Division were to arrive. However, it would not be before the evening of May 13 that the German division reached the outskirts of Rotterdam, and stuck there on one of the many canals. Unable to cross this, the Germans issued an ultimatum at 10.30 to the Dutch; either they surrender within two hours, or Rotterdam will be levelled to the ground by bombing. The ultimatum was rejected as it was unsigned. The next one followed at 13.20. Finally the Dutch decided to surrender, but their decision apparently came too late. Over 50 Heinkels of KG 54 were already on their way. According to the Germans, communications failed at this stage and the crews did not notice signal flares. The result was the destruction of the city centre and the death or wounding of some 900 people. The Dutch maintain that the order to carry out the raid was issued in cold blood by Goring himself, which does not however necessarily mean that the German version of events is totally untrue.

Two months of continuous fighting through May and June had cost the Germans 511 bomber aircraft (including reconnaissance versions), of which 438 were lost to enemy action. Of these, 264 (including 8 reconnaissance), i.e. almost 50% of the total figure, were He 111s, 233 of which were lost during the Battle of France to all reasons.

OVER ENGLAND

After conquering France, the Germans had only one aim, to eliminate Britain from the game. As a consequence of tactical errors, indecision and recklessness on the par Third Reich's leaders, the Battle of Britain was only fought in the air, and in an incompetent fashion, thereby raising the first questions as to the accuracy of the Douhet Theory, and bringing, ultimately, the first German defeat. The summer and autumn of 1940 was also a turning point for the Gfnter brothers design which started to give way to the Ju 88, its slightly more modern and flexible competitor. Despite this, thanks to its proven merits and versatility, Heinkel 111s played a major part in the Battle of Britain.

August 13, was the starting day of the decisive combats. On that day German bombers attacked airfields in the southern England, but as the fighting had continued since the beginning of July, and the British possessed a not bad early warning system and an excelent intelligence (Enigma), so there was no chance of surprise and the fight for domination in the air consisted mainly in shooting down British fighters in heavy battles. The heaviest attack was carried out by the Luftwaffe on August 15, and on that day Luftflotten 2, 3 and 5 lost the greatest number of aircraft, namely 79, including 12 He 111Hs and Ps. The greatest losses were inflicted on Stab, I, II/KG 26, sixty-three Heinkels of which were to attack targets in eastern Britain, after a long flight from Norway. The Geshwader was escorted by 34 Me 110s of I/ZG 76, but this did not suffice to prevent attacks by 4 British fighter squadrons, which caused the loss of 8 He 111H–4s and 8 Zerstörers for the loss of a single *Hurricane* (the RAF pilots claimed 25 bombers). Such high losses were an unpleasant surprise for the attackers, even more so as the earlier raids were not as costly. During the first day of the operation the Germans only lost 39 aircraft, in-

A He 111 H–5 of KG 53, summer 1941. There is a well visible MG FF cannon in the ventral pod.

cluding just 2 He 111s (only one, of III/KG 27, in action), while on August 14, the losses amounted to 18 aircraft, including 8 He 111s (6 of these in action). August 18, was the second worst day in terms of losses, the Luftwaffe losing then 69 aircraft, of these 9 were He 111s, in exchange for which the RAF paid 27 fighters lost in combat and 41 other aircraft (including 12 fighters) destroyed on ground. On the night of August 24, crews of III/KG 55 bombed London for the first time, the city becoming the principal target for German attacks two weeks later. In an ominous development on that same night, a Blenheim of 29 Squadron shot down an He 111.

The He 111 had a strong construction. At this photo a crew of a He 111H plane watching remains of a barrage balloon they collided with during night mission over England. Note missing frontal MG 17 gun.

(R. Michulec coll.)

Day by day the Germans strained British air defences, but the price they paid was high. The fighting was severe and inflicted heavy, ir- reparable losses, increasing at a frightening rate the number of unserviceable aircraft. On Sep- tember 7, the day the second stage of the Battle began, Luftflotten 2 and 3 possessed the follow- ing numbers of Heinkels:
Luftflotte 2:
●Sta' I, II, III/KG 1 — 50 serviceable/29 unser- viceable
●Stab, I, II/KG 4 — 51/33
●Stab, I, II/KG 26 — 17/40 (!)
●Stab, I, II, III/KG 53 — 33/43 (!)
●KGr 126 — 26/7
Luftflotte 3:
●Stab, I, II, III/KG 27 — 45/49 (!)
●KGr 100 — 7/21 (!)
●Stab, I, II, III/KG 55 — 68/20

Some 35 He 111s were allocated to the recon- naissance flights — 2, 3, 4, 5(F)/122; 1, 3(F)/121 and 1(F)/120. More than 20 were also used in other units as courier and liaison aircraft. Of course, the most important were the Heinkels in combat units where, as shown above, their num- ber reached 526 machines, of which 239 were unserviceable. No less than four units had more damaged than flyable aircraft, which surely must have represented one of the more critical mo- ment in early Luftwaffe history.

September 15, is generally accepted as the turning point in the Battle of Britain, and even though the question whether it really was 'turning' is still open, it is a matter of fact that it was the day of the heaviest fighting during that month. In 24 hours of combat, during which the Germans carried out 14 night missions (involv- ing 74 He 111s) and 8 day missions (involving 73 He 111s) they lost 56 aircraft, including 10 He 111s.

The best proof of the fierce and intense fight- ing over Britain is the fact that out of 25 He 111s claimed by the Poles in the RAF, no more than 5 could really be shot down. The worst from that viewpoint was September 26 in the afternoon encounter with 59 He 111s of KG 55 Greif on their way to bomb the *Spitfire* factory on the Solent. On the way the Luftwaffe formation was attacked by 3 British squadrons, the Polish 303 Squadron being one of these. After a long com- bat the Poles claimed the score of 9−1−1 [5], while in fact the 'Greif' wing only lost one He 111 shot down and another damaged on that day. The defenders failed to prevent the bombing which killed 89 people, destroyed three aircraft and damaged 20 more.

The last Heinkel bomber, lost over Britain during the Battle was an He 111H-3 of I/KG 1 missing in action near West Raynham on Oc- tober 29, 1940. This was the third (fifth accord- ing to the British) stage of the battle which gradually turned into night intruder missions lasting until the summer of 1941, and called by the British the 'Blitz'. Until that time (August — October 31) the Luftwaffe lost as many as 395 He 111s, of which 235 fell to enemy action.

NIGHT OPERATIONS OVER BRITAIN

Heinkel 111s played a major part in the night raids against Britain. They were so designed, and the H-5 variant prepared to carry such specialist weapon types, that some kinds of mission could only be performed by this type of aircraft. The products of Heinkel A.G. could carry heavy bombs, perform precise pinpoint attacks, act as pathfinders or simply function as basic bombers. At the time the Heinkel He 111 represented the nearest approach to a strategic bomber that the Luftwaffe possessed. The first raid was carried out on the night of November 1/2, 1940, by 80 Heinkels of KG 55 (against London) and 58 Heinkels of KGr 100 (against Birmingham). This

latter unit being a specialist unit with elite crews [7] carried out the most destructive attacks. It led a raid against Britain for the first time on the night of November 4/5, when 231 bombers attacked Liverpool and London. Again on the night of November 13, 18 He 111s of the group carried out the first precision attack against Coventry. They were followed by 437 further bombers heading for the fires started by the crews of KGr 100, and dropped 51,000 kg of bombs, turning the city into chaos. 554 people were killed, nearly a thousand wounded. Even though the raid was so heavy, it was only a beginning, as the night air war reached its climax in the spring of 1941. On the night of April 16/17, 685 bombers attacked London, flying 759 sorties, while on the night of April 19/20, 785 sorties were flown. The number of missions could be that high because some crews flew two or even three mission during one night. The first of these attacks lasted for 9 hours and caused 1179 deaths and 2233 wounded, and only cost the Germans 3 bombers, which to shoot down the RAF needed 164 night fighters. The second raid lasted 7 hours and was led by 13 He 111H–5y of III/KG 26 equipped with Y–Geräte. 1000 tonnes of bombs were dropped on the city and 101 RAF fighters accompanied by the AA batteries were only able to shoot down 2 German bombers (a He 111H–5 of 7/KG 4 was shot down by a *Hurricane* of 151 Squadron), while two more were lost to accidents. Practically the Germans acted with impunity since the British were not yet capable of efficently countering their night bombers (e.g. the special path finding unit of III/KG 26 'Löwen' lost only 4 He 111H–5y during last two months of 1940, only three of these falling to enemy action). The immunity ended in the spring of 1941 when the British were finally able to oppose and shoot down large numbers of aircraft using airborne radars. III Gruppe of the 'Löwen' Geshwader received the brunt in April, when in two nights they lost no less than 9 Heinkels, and on the night of May 3/4, three more machines. The last heavy raid of 507 bombers was carried out on May 10 against London. Then such actions were rendered impossible by the need to disperse forces to other parts of Europe.

Besides the massive, devastating raids against British cities, the Germans also attacked individual targets in the military industry. The Parnall factory at Yate where Bristol *Beaufighters* were manufactured was one such target. The first raid on February 22, was a failure as the He 111H–3 of III/KG 27 was shot down at Portbury. The next one, courageously carried out at an altitude of some 20 m by a single He 111 P–2 flown by Oblt. Hermann Lohmann of the II/KG 27 staff on 27th of that month, was a succcess. Subsequently, another attack against the same target was carried out, again by Lohmann, but with somewhat different results. Even though the crew managed to break through the defences again, and dropped 7 bombs on the target, only two of these exploded, and the machine was damaged, flying back on only one engine. It would seem that Lohmann declared his own private war on the factory, since he appeared there again on March 3, to drop bombs precisely and get back to France in a damaged aircraft. Probably, he might have continued this practice for longer, had his unit not been transferred to other duties.

OVER THE BALKANS

The rapidly developing war with Britain, as well as Mussolini's incompetence, forced Hitler to turn his attention towards the Balkans as early as autumn 1940, but it was not until the Yugoslav coup d'etat and the manifest inclination of

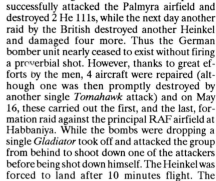

General Simovic to turn his country into another Soviet republic, that Hitler chose to react quickly. It took a mere 11 days from the coup d'etat until the Luftwaffe opened up yet another victorious campaign for the Third Reich, using 1131 aircraft — of which 299 were bombers, but only 30 of these were He 111s of II/KG 4. [8]

The first action in which the He 111P–4s of KG 4 'Gen. Wever' took part, was an attack against Belgrade, the Yugoslav capital, made on April 6 at 07:00 in the company of 160 KG 2 and KG 3 bombers. The Heinkels also took part in another raid against the city, contributing largely to its destruction and numerous victims among civilians. The next task on that day was to lay mines in the shipping lanes to the port of Piraeus, which was actually the units normal duty. This ended II/KG 4's operations over the Balkans as the battle for Yugoslavia ended 17, and Greece fell on April 23. Even before the end of hostilities II/KG 4 was transferred for minelaying duties in the eastern part of the Mediterranean, particularly over the Suez Canal, thus continuing the tasks of the 2 Staffel of the Geschwader that had carried out such duties, amongst others in this area, since mid-December 1940. On the night of May 5/6 1941 the crews of II Gruppe laid mines at Alexandria and the Suez Canal with no losses, but on May 8 a similar action by II/KG 26, also active in this area, ended in slaughter when the Germans were intercepted by the Fulmars of 806 FAA Squadron (from HMS *Formidable* escorting the 'Tiger' convoy) and lost 4 He 111Hs. Another Heinkel, this time of II/KG 4, was shot down in this region (on the night of May 17/18) by a *Hurricane* of 94 Squadron, its debris falling on a village and killing 6 Egyptians. Both Heinkel

Gruppen were also used, albeit to a small extent, during the invasion of Crete, when they attacked the airfields. II/KG 4 destroyed a Hurricane at Maleme on May 18, damaging two more with no losses, while a half-hearted attack of KG 26 against Heraklion ended in the destruction of 2 He 111s. During the Balkan campaign KG 4 lost two He 111s, and 5 more during the twelve missions over the eastern Mediterranean between May 1 and June 7. One of the downed crews had to sail in their dinghy for three days before being rescued by an Italian destroyer. Part of II/KG 26, during their five and a half month long stay at Rhodos, lost 7 He 111s, of which 6 were destroyed in the two actions described above. During that time the unit sank two ships, damaged another, and laid hundreds of mines.

OVER IRAQ

At the beginning of 1941 groups of Arab politicians began actions in Iraq with the aim of gaining independence from the British occupation, called diplomatically the British Colonial Mandate. It is not possible to determine the exact date when the rising broke out since the conflict developed gradually, but the first air actions took place on May 2, when a group of Wellingtons bombed Iraqi forces at Habbaniya. Seeing an opportunity to stretch British resources further, the Germans sent to Iraq a total of 14 Me 110s of ZG 26 and ZG 76, 7 [9] He 111 P–4s of 4./KG 4 and 20 Ju 52s and 2 Ju 90s to carry men and supplies. Oberst W. Junck was in command of the German force, and the bomber Staffel was commanded by Hptm. Schwanhausser. The first combat between the British and the Germans took place on May 13, but the Heinkels were in

trouble even before entering action. On May 14, at 18:00, a single Tomahawk of 250 Squadron successfully attacked the Palmyra airfield and destroyed 2 He 111s, while the next day another raid by the British destroyed another Heinkel and damaged four more. Thus the German bomber unit nearly ceased to exist without firing a proverbial shot. However, thanks to great efforts by the men, 4 aircraft were repaired (although one was then promptly destroyed by another single *Tomahawk* attack) and on May 16, these carried out the first, and the last, formation raid against the principal RAF airfield at Habbaniya. While the bombs were dropping a single *Gladiator* took off and attacked the group from behind to shoot down one of the attackers before being shot down himself. The Heinkel was forced to land after 10 minutes flight. The aircraft was lost, while the crew was able to escape to have a long and adventurous trip across this exotic country, ending with a week-long party with the representatives of the Arab authorities in Baghdad, to celebrate the happy ending of the story.

These three days practically ended the whole story of 4/KG 4 in the land of 'a thousand and one nights'. Lack of fuel, bombs, ammunition and spares, destruction of 5 He 111s, and bad organisation rendered the unit practically useless. On the way back, one of the He 111s had to land at Beirut in the Lebanon with one engine out, but friendly Frenchmen arranged a new engine within 24 hours and the last Heinkel left the Middle East.

OVER THE SOVIET UNION

For the war with the Soviet Union the Luftwaffe utilised over three Luftflotten, with the primary strike force consisting of 1251 bombers in 14 Geschwadern. Their principal equipment consisted of Ju 88s and Ju 87s, while He 111s were only used in the following units:
- Stab, I, II, III/KG 27
- Stab, I, II, III/KG 53 (the two units totalling in all some 180 Heinkel 111Hs)
- Stab, I, II, III/KG 55 — 104 He 111Ps
- II/KG 4 — 25 He 111P–4s

These units had a total of some 309 He 111s, while the total number of twin-engined bombers was 945.

During the first attacks against the Soviet airfields the Luftwaffe bomber units caused devastation on an unheard of scale. On the first day, with mass strafing and bombing attacks, some 1000 aircraft were destroyed on the ground, and during the first two weeks this number grew to almost 3500! Thousand of vehicles, hundreds of trains, dozens of ships fell victim to the bombers. The Kampfgeschwadern striking force was such that no unit, or defence line, no concentration of combat troops could withstand it. All Heinkel units were used for various tasks, with the exception of the II/KG 4 which, from July 4, was occupied solely with minelaying in the Black Sea. The 120 mines laid by the crews of the Gruppe sank 4 ships.

On July 19, 1941, Hitler issued a directive that raids on Moscow should be mounted in retaliation for Soviet attacks against Bucharest and Helsinki. Even though preparations ran quickly, the organisational problems and the need to reduce the means limited the number of participating bombers to 150, and the attacks consisted mainly of inaccurate bombing of political and military targets in Moscow and the surrounding area. 8 units were chosen for the raids, of which 6 flew He 111s. Four of these were transferred from Western Europe: KG 4 and KG

A He 111H–4 plane during flight over enemy territory, 1940.
(MAP)

28, and the pathfinding Gruppen, KGr 100 and III/KG 26. Two Geschwadern from the southern front sector were also detached: KG 54 and 55, while Luftflotte 2 chose KG 3 and KG 53. The first raid was carried out on the night of July 21/22, 1941 with 127 bombers. 35 He 111s of KG 53 led by Oberstleutnant Kohl were the crux of the action, since the Kremlin was their target. At first it seemed that the crews hit their target, but after a photo reconnaissance it turned out that the subject of the attack was a stadium. Never again was the seat of the Soviet authorities a target for German bombers. The next night 115 Heinkels went to Moscow; then on July 25/26, only 3, on 26/27, 65; of which one did not return (until that night the Soviet air defence — fighters, AA artillery, balloons — had claimed 48 German bombers destroyed at night). During August daytime attacks were started and even though these improved the bombing accuracy, the response of the Soviet defences improved as well. While the small attacks against Moscow on August 9 and 10 were successful, the August 11 raid of KGr 100 on one of the suburban factories brought the loss of two He 111s. In total, 76 raids were carried out against the city by the end of 1941 (122 according to the Soviets).

Two air raids against Stalingrad, on August 23, and September 3, 1942, can serve as examples of well organised and precisely carried out bombing. Ground support bombing attacks were carried over all that period, but the two carpet bombings, the first and the last, were the heaviest and wiped Stalingrad out as a city. No other European city has been as effectively destroyed by air attacks as the 'Stalin city'. Of 42,000 buildings, not a single one was left in condition that would permit habitation. The London experience compared to Stalingrad is like rain compared to a waterfall.

Apart from the Moscow raids, the most famous strategic action was the summer offensive against Soviet military industry in the June 1943. For this operation 13 bomber groups were chosen from KG 1, 3, 4, 27, 51, 55 and 100, with a total of 168 serviceable bombers, mainly He 111s. The first raid was carried out on the night of June 5/6 against the principal Gorki factories. Later Yaroslav and Saratov were also bombed with 149 bombers, of which 5 were lost. Subsequent raids were carried over a month with varying intensity, the majority of these were basically successful. In almost every case the bombing force was slightly larger than 100 aircraft, (the third raid involved 154 bombers, the fifth 132), though in some instances only several dozen machines or less attacked a target. The Soviets noticed more than 150 bombers only once, mostly their estimates did not exceed 80 aircraft in a raid. The raids involved prolonged flight time, up to 6 hours, and the necessity to pass the strong AA and fighter defence which caused general losses in the order of 15 – 20 He 111s. The targets were strongly protected, and after the third raid against Gorki the GKO decided to reinforce the defence of this centre with no less than 450 AA guns, 75 balloons and 100 searchlights. The Soviets maintained that during this June battle of factories they shot down a total of 40 bombers; 16 during 9 raids on Saratov and 14 in 7 Gorki raids. The attacks were not strong enough to stop production, but they caused a considerable slow down which led to a drop in production output of aircraft from 3100 during April and May to 2778 in June; and of armoured vehicles from 2303 – 1913 during March – May to 1481 in June.

The He 111H–4 or H–5 with a old style ventral pod, Russia 1941. The aircraft was coded NT+A... Note a non-standard fuselage camouflage and the partly overapinted cross.
(R. Michulec coll.)

Apart from these actions, He 111s also carried out devastating attacks against the Soviet airfields, often without losses as the Soviets did not bother to protect their bases with AA artillery. One of the more successful actions was KG 4's attack against the Kursk — East airfield on the night of March 21/22, 1943, after which the crews claimed 35 single-engined aircraft, and of the remaining 25 Hurricanes only 2 escaped undamaged. Besides victories, losses happened as well. Only seven months earlier one of the Gruppen of this Geschwader lost 3 Heinkels during a Soviet attack against the airfield at Seshchinskaya, and 15 more were severely damaged. I/KG 100 dealt well with Soviet shipping and ground targets in the Crimea, operating from early 1942 from the Saki airfield. During February and March the crews of the Gruppe sank 2 ships and a submarine [10], but on the night of February 21/22, two Soviet destroyers shelled their airfield and the unit lost 4 He 111s, while 17 more were damaged. A similar situation was repeated on the night of March 20/21 but the Soviet shells only seriously damaged 5 Heinkels.

One of the most spectacular actions of the German Geschwadern was a night attack carried out during summer 1944. In the afternoon of June 21, 163 US 8th AF B–17s landed at Poltava and Mirogrod. They were shadowed by German aircraft and a few hours later the Germans attacked them successfully. The night attack against Ukrainian airfields involved some 100 He 111s each of KG 53 b Poltava and KG 55 b Mirogrod, led by two teams each of 8 He 111H–16/R3s of III/KG 4. During the approach to the targets the weather at Mirogrod proved bad so both formations attacked Poltava to devastate it completely. 44 B–17s and 5 other aircraft were destroyed, while 26 B–17s and 28 other aircraft were damaged. 400,000 litres of aircraft fuel were also set ablaze.

An important part of the Luftwaffe bomber units duties was delivering supplies. This was carried out for the first time in the late winter/early spring 1942 in the forests of northern Russia, south of the Ilmen lake. Two (of three) principal towns of the region, Demyansk and Velke Luki, were encircled by the Soviets. The Germans broke through to the first of these and were air-supplied until spring 1943, but Velke Luki was never relieved. The air supplies by three Heinkel Gruppen of KG 4 and KG 53, and Go 242 gliders, came to nothing and after 55 days of bitter fighting the troops surrendered. Throughout the nearly two months of the action both Geschwadern lost 17 He 111s and 11 gliders, and one of the crews, that of Hptm. Lehmann, shot down behind enemy lines, made 40 km in two days to get back to their own lines!

The air bridge to Stalingrad was a much more bitter failure. When the second stage of the most tragic WWII battle opened, Luftflotte 4 had only one transport Gruppe equipped with Heinkels, the KGr zbV 5, operating in this section of the front since summer 1942. Some combat Heinkels were also detached for transport duties, mainly the He 111H–6, H–11 and H–16 that enabled external attachment of loads under the fuselage. These came from I/KG 100, II/KG 26, III/KG 4, I, II/KG 27 and Stab, I, II, III/KG 55. All the Heinkel-equipped groups were gathered into an ad hoc unit called 'Transportfliegerführer 1' (unit represents a corps level) and given over to the command of Oberst Kohl. On January 24, 1942 Luftflotte 4 possessed 355 He 111s, including 159 for transport duties, but only 55 were serviceable.

Weather conditions often rendered the Stalingrad supply missions impossible and contributed to heavy losses and low serviceability; for example, on November 19, of only 21 volunteers crews, only 13 reached Stalingrad. For the same reasons He 111s were often the only aircraft able to supply the encircled units, even though there were twice as many specialised transport aircraft. Again, on December 8, it was 70 He 111s that brought the major portion of supplies, and on the 19th of the month, 73 He 111s carried 146 tonnes of goods to Stalingrad, while 63 other aircraft brought 143 tonnes. Many

One of the 9 He 111H–6 planes received by the FARR, 1944.

(Bernád Denés coll.)

crews of the 'Spades' performed extraordinary achievements, two of which became widely known. Feldwebel Jackstat of I/KG 100 flew 4 missions to the Stalingrad pocket and back in 24 hours, and Oberleutnant G. Roth, the CO of 5./KG 55 took 25 wounded soldiers on board, even though the standard load for an He 111 was 15 men.

To try to save the ever worsening situation, early January 1943 saw the formation of six new KGr zbVs, (Transport units), four of which, KGr zbV 20, 23, 24 and 25 were equipped with 162 He 111E's, F's and H's. These machines, together with their crews, were taken from various flying schools and institutions, but none of them was employed in action, and after the fall of Stalingrad they were all disbanded. The same happened to the KGr zbV 5, formed in March 1942 from the crews gathered from flying schools for the Demyansk action, which was reformed in summer 1943 into I/KG 55. It was replaced by KGr zbV 30 equipped with He 111Hs. During the Stalingrad fighting between November and February, Luftflotte 4 lost 165 He 111s, mainly due to accidents, while the Soviets claimed 138 Heinkels during that time.

Stalingrad does not end the story of the transport Heinkels. On the contrary, their importance

started to grow slowly and the R2 modification to the He 111 made it the principal glider towing and cargo type. He 111s served in all paratroop units, towed gliders in six Go 242 Staffeln from the turn of 1941, and later, from 1943, formed 40 – 80% of the towing equipment in four Schleppgruppen equipped with Go 242's and DFS 230's. These units took part in all great and small supply operations in eastern and western Europe, supported by two glider Geschwadern, LLG 1 and LLG 2, which also used He 111s. Both arrived at Stalingrad, but too late to affect the course of events. The LLG 1, which arrived at the front in early January 1942, possessed two Gruppen equipped entirely with He 111s and Go 242s, while the I/LLG 2 (at the front since late December 1942) had 14 Ju 88s, Do 17s and He 111s plus 82 gliders. After the fall of Paulus' 6th Army both Geschwadern were employed over Kuban, from where they were withdrawn in mid-spring and moved to other sections of the Eastern Front or other regions of Europe. At the end 1943 the LLG 2 was reformed and re-equipped entirely with 31 He 111s and 265 Go 242s. As well as TGr 30 (ex-KGr zbV 30), Heinkels were probably also a part of the equipment of TGr 20, and by the end of the war the KG 4 and KG 28 bomber Geschwadern were also used for

transport duties, using the R2 modification Heinkels [11]. The transport and glider units played a major part in winter and spring of 1944 in the Ukraine, during the battles of Cherkassy and Kamenets Podolsky, where large German forces were cut off. During the first of these battles the Germans lost 45 transport aircraft (including 13 He 111s), but they evacuated almost 2300 wounded and supplied 2026 tonnes of supplies. In the second, thanks to supplies of fuel and ammunition dropped by the units under Transportfliegerführer 2, a large group of the Germans broke through to their own lines. The TFF 2 had under his command, apart from SlGr 2 and TGr 30 on 111s, also (like at Stalingrad) I/KG 4 and Gruppen of KG 54 and KG 55. Operating in extremely difficult conditions, the transport units performed their tasks with relatively low losses (e.g. TGr 30 lost 4 He 111s and delivered 1487 tonnes of supplies). The greatest success of that year was achieved in April and May, during the Crimean airlift. During this operation aircraft evacuated 21,500 men out of Sevastopol, for the loss of 60 machines. During these supply operations no less than 500 transport aircraft were in continuous use use on the southern section of the front.

The Breslau (now Wrocław, Poland) airlift lasted until the end of the war and cost the Germans no less than 165 aircraft, but for this price the soldiers could fight until May 6, 1945. The transport Heinkels flew 503 sorties in that operation and supplied some 500 tonnes which was equal to 56% of the Ju 52 contribution. It was different was the case of Posen (Poznań). Almost 100 transport aircraft flew 169 missions, delivering almost 260 tonnes of supplies and evacuating 235 wounded, but the the defence was not as strong as that at Breslau, and after a month of fighting and supplies (between January 28 and February 23, 1945) Posen fell on February 23. During February and March the He 111s (and Jus) also supplied Arnswalde and Glogau (Głogów) and helped Germans from the Pomerania region break through across the Oder to Germany. They also supported and evacuated the cut-off coastal garrisons in France and on the Baltic Sea, as well as Budapest.

The He 111Z *Zwilling* (Twins) also played a large part in supply operations. The story started in early 1942, when they arrived in three glider Gruppen equipped with Me 321s. Two of these acted independently, while the third was III Gruppe LLG 1. III/LLG 1 arrived at Stalingrad in late January 1943, but was soon transferred south to Kuban, where the GSKdo 1 and 2 were already based. The former had 22 *Gigants* and 3 He 111Zs, the latter 15 Me 321 and 4 He 111Zs. In early spring all *Zwillings* at Luftwaffe disposal arrived at the front, together with some 45 Me 321s. Like other units, these too were transferred in the summer 1943 to other parts of Europe,

At this photo is clearly visible moment of He 111H–6 plane engines worming-up. Note missing frontal MG FF/M cannon, a fix for MG 15 over cannon and two bomb racks.

(MVT via M. Krzyżan)

The He 111H–11/R2, W.Nr 8433 captured by Americans in France, 1944. This aircraft belonged probably to TGr 30.

(R. Michulec coll.)

mainly to Southern France and Italy, where they co-operated with General Student's paratroopers in the fighting. They appeared again in the East in the summer 1944, and there their story ended. Because all *Gigants* were destroyed or damaged beyond repair, the He 111Zs were transferred to Schleppgruppen where they worked until the end of the war, towing 3 Go 242s at one time. Of the twelve Zwillings only 4 survived the war.

When discussing He 111 activities in the Eastern Front we should not forget their role in fighting the Soviet night bombers. The attacks of U–2 (Po–2) light bombers during summer 1942 made the Luftwaffe headquarters organise units destined specifically to counter that threat. It was decided that against this secondary enemy a small force of five Nachtjagdschwarmen would be directed, these reporting directly to the commanders of Luftflotten and would be equipped mainly with He 111s of various subtypes, armed additionally with four 20 mm cannon. After the front line was rebuilt in February 1943, 3 of the 5 disorganised Schwarmen were resurrected and transferred to Luftflotte 1, LwKdo 'Don' and 'Ost'. Because of increasing night attacks their importance grew steadily, so after 6 He 111s, a Ju 88C–6 and a Me 110 formed the initial equipment of the three units, from April 1943, 22 more aircraft arrived. Prior to the Kursk Battle the name was changed to Nahnachtjagdschwarmen and they were transferred to the area of the planned battle, where they operated extensively, shooting down 30 Soviet aircraft by July 1943. After Operation Zitadelle (the Battle of Kursk), in early August the NNJSch were disbanded and reformed into two full size night fighter units, the NJG 100 and NJG 200. At the end of August the last, eighth, flight of II Gruppe NJG 200 was formed with the last six crews of NNJSch with 3 He 111s and 3 other aircraft. The Heinkels served in these Geschwadern for a few months only, until they were transferred to bomber units, being replaced with specialised He 111 H–20s, serving in the role of air command posts.

Apart from the fighter, the He 111 with additional cannon armament also performed a standart for this models anti-railway duties. These consisted in deep intrusions into enemy-held territory and destroying the trains with cannon fire. Such duties were performed by special Staffeln in bomber units starting from early 1942, and these continued until the end of the war. The anti-railway units operated within the following Geschwadern: 14(eis)/KG 27 from 1942, using He 111s until early 1943 (later reformed as a heavy fighter unit); 14 (eis)/KG 3 from 1942 (in

Two Americans posed before a He 111H–10 or H–11. It could be the same aircraft which was later sent to USA for tests (W.Nr. 8433).

the beginning as 6(eis) on Ju 88s); 7(eis)/KG 51, from early 1943 on Ju 88; 9(eis)/KG 55 from early 1943, at first with Ju 88s, later reformed as 14(eis) and re-equipped with He 111s; 14(eis)/KG 4 from 1942 with He 111s.

OVER THE SEAS

The greatest achievements by He 111s resulted from the activities of KG 4 and the anti-shipping missions flown by KG 26 in the Mediterranean and the Arctic.

Late 1940 moved the central point of the fighting from the British coasts to the Mediterranean where a whole British–German war was to be fought. The first Heinkels appeared there in December 1940 within Fliegerkorps X. Of 307 aircraft there were 55 He 111s, including 48 He 111H–4s of II/KG 26 for minelaying and bombing of maritime targets. To support the corps in the eastern part of the sea, 2./KG 4 was transferred for similar duties to Rhodes, later joined by a part of II/KG 26. The first success of II Gruppe came on January 31, 1941, when they managed to track down a group of British ships and sink a merchant and a naval ship, and damage another merchant ship. From mid-1941 their activities ceased because of the transfer of the unit to other duties, but then the 6 Staffel of KG 26 appeared again, joined by two more Staffeln of II/KG 26, I/KG 100 (transferred to the eastern Mediterranean) and III/KG 26 (but this on Ju 88s). Increasing Allied sea activity in this region gave Heinkel crews a lot of work. On August 12, 1942, seven He 111s attacked a convoy and sank 2 ships, while damaging a third. During Operation 'Torch' (from November 7, the same year), the Allied defence was so strong that no successes were achieved, even though there were plenty of targets. To increase the Luftwaffe force in Italy, I/KG 26 was also transferred there, with their He 111 H–6s, achieving their first success on November 18, 1942, when

a ship was sunk. On November 15 the Geschwader had only 74 bombers, and until June 1943 these (without the II Gruppe) sank 8 ships and damaged 10 more. During the Tunisian fighting (November 1, 1942 – March 13, 1943) air elements sank 33 ships (of the total of 91), in this the KG 26 aircraft accounted for 10, i.e. some 30%.

After the fall of Tunisia the anti-shipping activities were of the long range type, mainly because of the Allied air superiority. The day of Sicily invasion (July 10) saw only 24 He 111s in Stab and I/KG 26, and even these were soon transferred to southern France and temporarily included in FlD 2. During their missions over the Algerian coast, the He 111s, together with Ju 88s of III/KG 26, sank 10 more ships (until the end of 1943), and by mid-1944 the four Gruppen of KG 26 and KG 77 had sunk 10 more ships and damaged 3. That was to be one of their last victories.

From late autumn 1941 convoys with Allied supplies started to arrive in Murmansk, these being soon discovered by the Germans who in the spring of 1942 attempted (not without success) to prevent them. The first engagement took place in late April and ended with the torpedoing and sinking of 3 Allied merchant ships from the PQ-15 convoy by He 115s of KuFlGr 906. The first organised attempt to destroy a convoy was undertaken between May 25–30, 1942. Serious air-sea combats took place on May 26, when 19 He 111s of I/KG 26 and 6 Ju 88s of III/KG 30 seriously damaged 2 ships, but it would take a day more before the real hell broke loose. Of 108 bombers that took part on the attack, only 7 were He 111s of II/KG 26 'Löwen', but of 6 ships sunk two fell to the torpedoes of the 'Lions'. Of 35 ships on the PQ-16 convoy 7 were sunk, and 5 more were damaged (including the Polish destroyer ORP 'Garland'). 147 tanks, 77 aircraft and 770 vehicles did not reach their destination, losses equivalent to a heavy land battle.

Another convoy, the PQ–17, was discovered soon after it sailed out to the sea and on July 2 it

No comments. Benina airfield, Benghazi. Libya.

(Ł. Ulatowski)

In September 1944 the last two production He 111s were delivered (of 120 bombers manufactured during that month for the Luftwaffe) thus bringing to an end the eight-year long production run. Of 19 bomber Gruppen on He 111s in May 1944, only 5 were left in January 1945, 4 of these within KG 4. This Geschwader had 87 He 111s on strength on January 10, the number dropping dropping to 33 in early April and increasing to 76 on April 25 (almost all the R2 modification). When the war ended the type was still operational also with Schleppgruppe 1 (15 He 111s, 14 other aircraft and 19 gliders) and TGr 30 (16 He 111s).

The last He 111 to be shot down in WWII fell to a pair of Soviet Yaks at Melnik in Bohemia on May 8, 1945.

AIRCRAFT GENERAL EVALUATION

The general opinion of the aircraft is decidedly favourable. It was easy and safe, both to fly and to handle. The crews liked the machine and were often not happy when it was replaced by its successor, the Ju 88. Heinkels could fly on one engine without problems, provided there was no serious damage. The sturdy construction could withstand even several hits with 20 mm rounds. These, and other advantages, earned the aircraft the name of 'licence to live'. During the early period of the war this was the best bomber of the Luftwaffe and its unquestionable position was held until 1945, even though it was rather thanks to the Third Reich's armament policy than to its own merits. Along with the bomber Ju 88, of which 9000 machines were built, the He 111 was the principal Luftwaffe bomber during WWII.

NOTES

[1] In fact only 300 people were killed due to the bombing, and the very act of bombing is somewhat debatable. The communist propaganda made it a war crime showpiece, the number of victims increasing several times. The Italian 205 Squadriglia was also involved in the Guernica attack.

[2] The list does not include an He 111 destroyed by saboteurs.

[3] Charles Lindbergh, the American transatlantic flyer, was greatly impressed by the Luftwaffe, and may even have had pro-nazi sympathies. He was an undoubted supporter of the Douhet Theory. His activities in the autumn of 1938 were priceless to the Germans.

[4] The He 111 was the most famous bomber of that time, mainly because of its proven effectiveness in Spain. For the general public it was a symbol of the Guernica and Barcelona massacres (the latter — 3300 victims). Thus every German bomber was generally considered to be an He 111.

[5] 9 kills — 1 probable — 1 damaged.

[6] The X–Geräte was first used in the summer 1940 by KGr 100, but not until the autumn did KGr 100 use it as a specialised pathfinding device for a large number of aircraft. The Y–Geräte also appeared with KG 26 in August, but the III Gruppe did not achieve operational capability before October.

[7] This is the general view of the historians. However, the 'elite' quality of the unit could only be applied to its early period. In fact, later on, some of the Gruppe's crews were rather inferior to those of other units.

[8] KG 4 was at that time another, next to KG 26, specialised unit for anti-shipping operations. The I Gruppe operated at that time over the Bay of Biscay, the III against sea (and ground) targets in Britain, while the 2nd Staffel over the Mediterranean, from Italian bases.

[9] 8 He 111s, out of the 9 planned for the action, arrived at Athens, from were the operation was to take place. Only 7 were able to take off from there. All the He 111s were de-modified to a standard bomber version capable of carrying 50 kg bombs in internal bomb bays.

[10] The Germans identified it as the SC–213 (rather Sh–213 in Russian) which was in fact sunk on October 10, 1942 at Constance. In fact it was Sh–210 that fell their victim.

[11] Both units, as the only ones in the Luftwaffe which flew throughout the war on He 111s.

[12] The III Gruppe also had 15 Ju 88s. All the data refers to serviceable aircraft, e.g. KG 4 had a total of 137 bombers, including 38 Ju 88s.

was attacked by the He 115s. On July 3 two attacks by He 111s sank 7 ships, the next day 3 more, these being hit by the crews of II/KG 26 (including 2 in co-operation with U-boats). On July 5 another 8 ships were the prey of KG 30 and KG 26 (including 2 in co-operation with U-boats). During the next few days the aircraft sank 2 more ships (one finished off by a U-boat) which brought the total to 23 out of 36 ships in the convoy, and for the loss of just 5 bombers. 3350 vehicles, 210 aircraft and 430 tanks went to the sea, not to mentioned the heavy loss of life.

The PQ-18 convoy was found by the Germans in early September, but this time the British drew conclusions from the previous disaster and the ships were accompanied by HMS 'Avenger' an escort carrier with 15 *Sea Hurricanes* on board. The first encounters of the naval aircraft with ships happened on September 8, but the first heavy attack was carried out six days later. Following previous experience the 'Lions' flew to their target in a large formation of 44 He 111s, and shortly before reaching the convoy they split and attacked it from all sides. The defence was extremely strong and only half of the crews managed to drop their torpedoes at a decent distance, but nevertheless after their attack 8 ships were sunk for the loss of 5 Heinkels (the sailors claimed 15 German aircraft). In spite of the relatively high losses, the attack was repeated the next day, but this time British fighters were awaiting the intruders. A prolonged combat resulted in 5 bombers shot down and 9 damaged beyond repair. The attacks continued until September 20, but these resulted in only 2 ships being hit, one sinking the other surviving the damage. Of the 10 ships sunk, 7 were destroyed solely by I and II/KG 26, albeit at the cost of 20 Heinkel 111s and 14 crews.

The September battle was the last on this convoy route since the situation in other theatres and the successes of the Allies forced the Germans to give up their efforts to stop the Arctic convoys. During the three great air-sea battles of 1942 the Luftwaffe sank almost 30 ships (nearly 10 of these in co-operation with U-boats) for the loss of 30 aircraft.

OVER EUROPE

The final countdown for the Third Reich's last year commenced in May 1944. The German army was in defence in all fronts, the Luftwaffe statistics being the best proof to that. In mid-1940 the Luftwaffe possessed 1464 fighters compared to 1808 bombers, while on May 31, 1944 there were 1730 fighters and only 841 bombers,

of which 435 were He 111s. A further 45 aircraft of the type were in reconnaissance and transport units (excluding the glider units). The He 111 was still the basic equipment for 19 bomber Gruppen (of 45 in existence, 21 of which still used Ju 88s), and production of the type reached 100 in that month, while only 250 of the other bombers were manufactured! In May the following units still used He 111s:

- III/KG 3 — 35 He 111
- II, IV/KG 27 — 54 He 111
- IV/KG 53 — 39 He 111
- IV/KG 55 — 34 He 111
- I/KG 100 — 15 He 111
- FAGr 123 — 6 He 111
  In the East:
- 14./KG 55 — 11 He 111
- Stab/SG 3 — 1 He 111
- I/KG 4 — 34 He 111
- I, II, III/KG 53 — 108 He 111
- NASt 1 — 6 He 111
- II, III, IV/KG 4 — 109 He 111
- I, III, 14./KG 27 — 90 He 111
- I, II, III/KG 55 — 101 He 111
- TGr 30 — 33 He 111

In spite of such great numbers of Heinkels, they were little used. In the West most Gruppen equipped with the type were training or replacement units for other bomber Geschwadern and did not take part in combat. The only action carried out with the type was attacking Britain with Fi 103 (V1) flying bombs from mid-1944. At first, from early July, such attacks were carried out by III/KG 3 under Major M. Better and later, in November, the whole of KG 53 was transferred to these duties, being however, rarely used in its full strength because of the fuel shortage. At first there were practically no losses, but as the weather deteriorated and the Allied counter-actions increased, these rose at a terrible rate. In early January KG 53 had 101 He 111H–22s, of which in just a few weeks 77 were lost, only 16 these to enemy action. Both the losses and the economic side of the activities were completely out of proportion to the effects, since the Fi 103s released from He 111s showed a lamentably low accuracy. The Soviets claiming that this type of the He 111 was used against bridgehead at Oder (Odra) river in early Spring of 1945 too.

In the Western Europe one of the last combats with He 111s was over Southern France when at August 19, 1944, 4 F6F of VOF-1 shot down 2 He 111 Hs of I/KG 4. Two of the Americans (Sandor and Robinson) killed a crew of one of the He 111s which tried to escape after a force landing.

TECHNICAL DESCRIPTION

Above: The He 111H–2s or H–3s in the mass production assembly line (W.Nr 3510 – 3530).

(R. Michulec coll.)

Fuselage

Semi–monocoque, all–metal, with oval cross–section. Built on 27 frames and 4 longerons, duralumin (alloy with magnesium) skinning flush–riveted to the structure. The fuselage was cigar–shaped and divided into three major portions: the crew cockpit; the bomb compartment, and the gunners compartment. The first of these was completely glazed and included the pilot–captain and navigator–bombardier–gunner seats. Behind the cockpit the bomb compartment was placed, separated from the rest the fuselage with double metal walls, with cut–outs enabling the crew members to move around the whole fuselage. In the middle portion of the fuselage, positioned directly on the wing axis, two vertical bomb bays were placed, consisting of 8 ESAC 250/IX cassettes installed on both sides of the compartment, fixed to the fuselage sides. Further to the rear another crew compartment was placed, for the two (later three) gunners. The upper gunner position was in the opening in the fuselage top skinning, and consisted of a steel structure, on which a steel gun ring was mounted with a seat fixed to it. Over nearly the entire length of this compartment a ventral cupola was attached which formed the ventral gun position as well as the uncomfortable entrance hatch for the whole crew. The same entrance served also for evacuation of the two (later three) gunners. Between the cupola and the bomb compartment wall the ventral gunner/radio–operator's position was placed, where he operated the radio set installed at the starboard side of the fuselage. The rear portion of the fuselage enclosed the semi–retractable tail wheel bay, and further aft, between the controls, an empty space covered with a fairing. In later series this mounted glider towing attachments (short stiff, or long elastic) or MG 17 guns.

Below: The last stage of assembling of a He 111H/P fuselage with frontal cockpit.. Note an angular bottom-right 'corner' of a circular frame of 'Ikaria' turret.

(R. Michulec coll.)

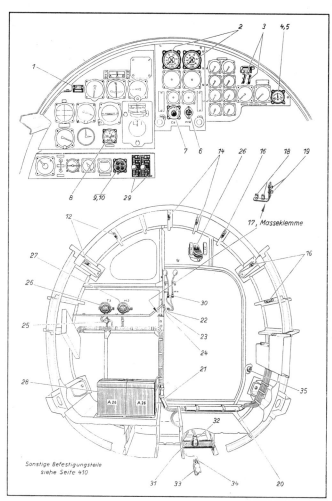

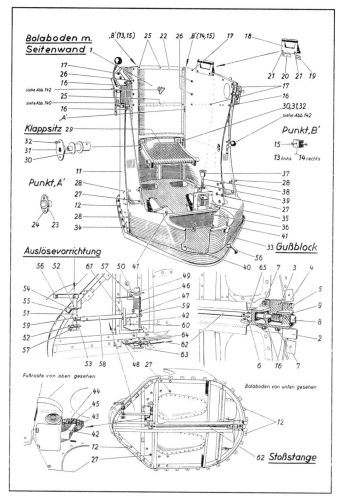

Bolaboden m. Seitenwand 1

siehe Abb.142

siehe Abb.140

Klappsitz 29

Punkt,A'

Auslösevorrichtung

Fußraste von oben gesehen

Bolaboden von unten gesehen

Punkt,B'

13 links   14 rechts

33 Gußblock

62 Stoßstange

Sonstige Befestigungsteile siehe Seite 410

17, Masseklemme

The parts of a original He 111 manual. Top left: The pilot's main control panel of the first generation He 111; B, D, E, F, J versions, and (below) a pass in the fuselage to the navigator cockpit. Above: The retractable gun position in He 111 B, D, E, F, J versions.

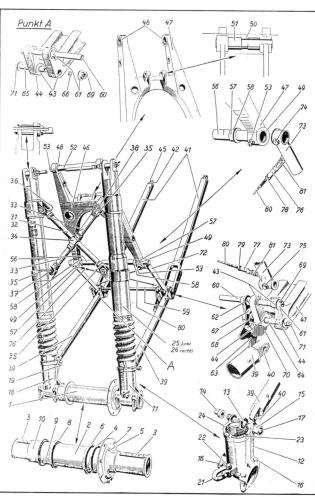

Punkt A

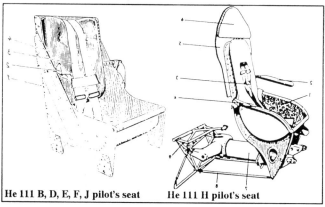

He 111 B, D, E, F, J pilot's seat   He 111 H pilot's seat

At the left: The details of the main landing gear's leg of the B to H–3 models. Later versions had slightly different, strengthened legs.

At the right: The tail wheel of the He 111. In the later models a spring cylinder (no '7' on the drawing) has replaced the elastic cord.

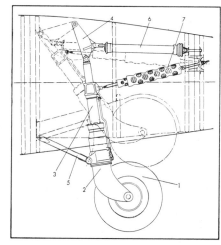

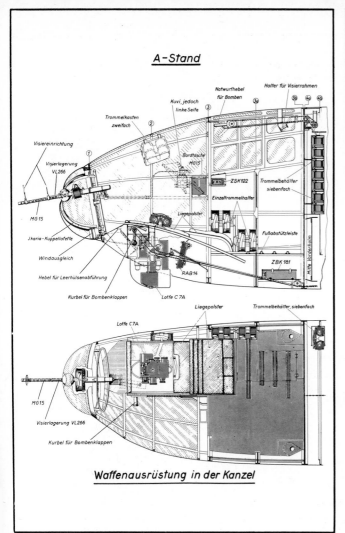

A-Stand

Visiereinrichtung
Visierlagerung VL266
MG 15
Jkaria-Kuppellafette
Windausgleich
Hebel für Leerhülsenabführung
Kurbel für Bombenklappen
Trommelkasten zweifach
Kuvi, jedoch linke Seite
Notwurfhebel für Bomben
Halter für Visierrahmen
Bordtasche MG15
ZSK122
Einzeltrommelhalter
Liegepolster
Loffe C 7A
RAB14
Trommelbehälter siebenfach
Fußabstützleiste
ZBK 181
Mitte Vorderholm

Loffe C 7A
Liegepolster
Trommelbehälter siebenfach
MG15
Visierlagerung VL266
Kurbel für Bombenklappen

Waffenausrüstung in der Kanzel

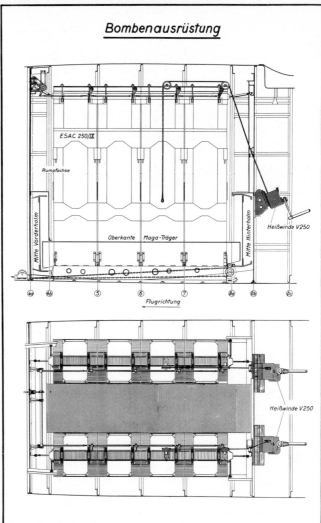

Bombenausrüstung

ESAC 250/II
Rumpfache
Mitte Vorderholm
Oberkante Maga-Träger
Mitte Hinterholm
Heißwinde V250
Flugrichtung
Heißwinde V250

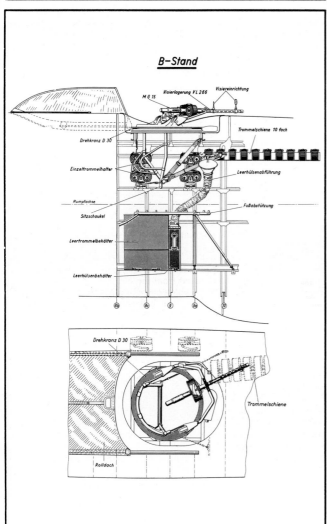

B-Stand

MG 15
Visierlagerung VL 266
Visiereinrichtung
Drehkranz D 30
Einzeltrommelhalter
Rumpfache
Sitzschaukel
Leertrommelbehälter
Leerhülsenbehälter
Trommelschiene 10 fach
Leerhülsenabführung
Fußabstützung

Drehkranz D 30
Trommelschiene
Rolldach

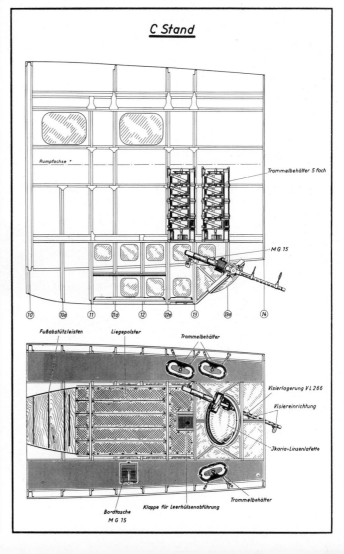

C Stand

Rumpfache
Trommelbehälter 5 fach
MG 15

Fußabstützleisten
Liegepolster
Trommelbehälter
Visierlagerung VL 266
Visiereinrichtung
Jkaria-Linsenlafette
Bordtasche MG 15
Klappe für Leerhülsenabführung
Trommelbehälter

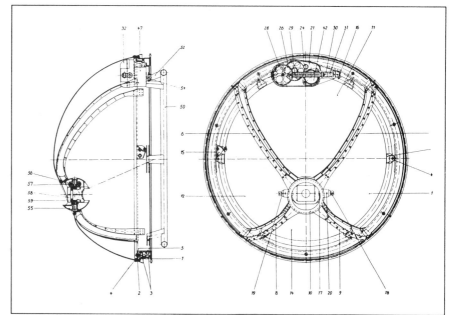

Above: The 'Ikaria' turret with MG 17.
At the right: A part of original manual documentation with a drawing of the same turret.

Wing

All–metal, three–section, two–spar. The rectangular centre section, with a characteristic cutout near the fuselage, enclosed fuel tanks, and had engine mountings fixed to the fore spar. The tapered outer wings, with rounded tips featured metal, fabric covered ailerons which worked together with flaps when deflected by more than 15 degrees. The flaps, covering the entire span of the wing centre section and the outer wing panels, were of the slotted type, metal–covered. All three portions of the wing were duralumin covered and flush–riveted like the fuselage. Moreover, both outer wings enclosed fuel tanks and signalling lamps, and the port wing incorporated pitot tube and landing light.

Tail

Both the vertical and horizontal surfaces were of cantilever type with elliptic planform and all–metal construction, covered and riveted in a way similar to the rest of the airframe. The horizontal surface AoA could be ground–adjusted in three ranges: high angle (-1.5 degrees), standard, and extra low angle ($-4,5$ degrees) for the machines without load or tail armament. The rudder was mass–balanced, while the elevators were mass– and aerodynamic-balanced at 20%.

Landing gear

Consisted of two main wheels with 1100 x 375 mm tyres, main wheel track 5,3 m, completely retractable into engine nacelles. They were mounted on double Faudi legs with pneumatic shock absorbers and hydraulic brakes. The tail wheel with 465 x 165 mm tyre, was fork mounted in the rear fuselage.

Systems

Fuel system consisted of two fuel tanks, of 700 litres each, in the wing centre section, and two tanks of 1025 litres each, in the outer wing panels. The 87 octane B4 grade fuel was electrically fed, or manually in emergency. Behind the engines filters were fitted and the valves to cut out fuel in case of fire. Some aircraft featured an additional 837 litre fuel tank in the port bomb bay which worked in a way similar to the integral tanks. In many versions the fuel system was modified to allow use of external drop tanks on outer pylons.

Oil system included two 190 litre tanks placed in the wing centre section, next to the fuel tanks. Oil was fed manually.

An oxygen system was installed in the fuselage and consisted of four (later five) sets of six spherical oxygen bottles each. All these were connected to make one system divided with four

Above: The DB 600G engine on display in the Aviation Museum in Cracow, Poland.

Below: The Jumo 211A engine on display in the Aviation Museum in Cracow, Poland.

(both R. Michulec)

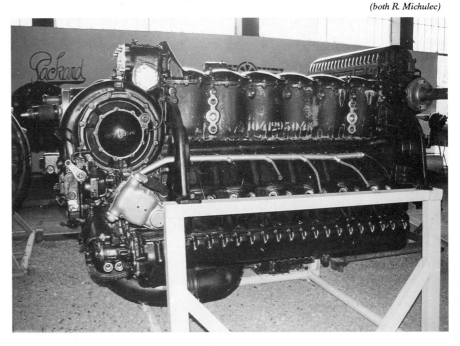

Another photo of a special PVC rack, this time with a supply containers of 700 kg.

A PVC bomb rack — 'table top' — on the He 111H-11, ordinary used in this model. On the rack are visible two 1000 kg bombs and 'free fingers' of another bomb racks.

(R. Michulec coll.)

(five) valves, and filled through one point. The main hydraulic system was used to adjust the pilot's seat, operate flaps, landing gear, and glycol coolers. The fluid was fed by a pump powered from the starboard engine, or in case of its failure, by a hand pump in the crew compartment.

Electrical system was twin-wire and screened type, 24V, fed by two Bosch generators rated at 1200 (or 2000) kW. Both were powered by the engines. The system also comprised two Varta batteries placed under the floor of the bomb compartment.

Engines

Two DB 601, weighting 610 kg, for the P variant, or two Jumo 211 (Jumo 213 in the final models) weighting 635 kg, driving metal or wooden VDM or Junkers–Hamilton HPC propellers, 3.4 m in diameter.

Armament

At first the bombers were armed only with three 7.9 mm MG 15 machine guns, later replaced with MG 17, MG 81 or MG 81Z (of the same calibre), MG FF 20 mm cannon or 13 mm MG 131 heavy machine guns. In the first versions the guns were placed in three positions, and were manned by three men, later five additional stations were added, of which one was finally removed, and a single additional crew member to man two of these. Standard armament included a maximum of 8 guns covering the whole space around the bomber. In the special versions the offensive weapons were assisted by four 20 mm MG FF or MG 151/20 cannon placed under the starboard wing centre section, and to the starboard of the pilot.

Bombs were carried in the internal bomb bays (maximum of 2000 kg) or on various under fuselage adapters (maximum 3000 kg). The contents of bomb bays could be dropped individually or in a salvo (by the bombardier) or in series (by the RAB 14d automatic device).

Radio equipment

Only the standard radio set of a standard bomber will be described here due to lack of space. This consisted of the FuG III wireless

The dorsal gun position with very well visible gunner armour protection.

(later replaced by FuG X) composed of two receivers, a transmitter, and two aerials — one above the fuselage (between the mast and the fin), and another trailed by the bomber under the fuselage.

Moreover, the aircraft were fitted with the FuBl-1 radio–navigation set, the aerial of which was placed inside the aerial mast on top of the fuselage, and the other under the fuselage. Peil G 5 radiofinder was also fitted, with the aerial under the gunner's fairing. In the P-1 and early H-1 series the radiofinder aerial was positioned behind the upper gunner position. From 1940 on, the set was modified and added to by various devices for radio–navigation and identification, and finally radars.

The frontal part of the H-10 or H-11 cockpit. The MG FF and the Kuto-Nase installation are clearly visible.

Below: The MG FF installed in the frontal part of the ventral pod.

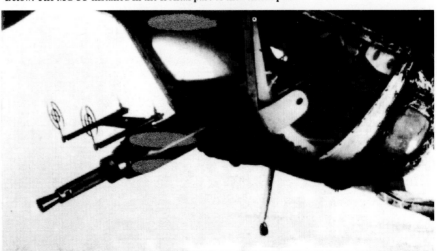

HEINKEL 111 SPECIFICATION

Type	He 111 V1	He 111 A–0	He 111 B–1 early	He 111 B–1 late	He 111 B–2	He 111 D–0
Dimensions: Span	25,00 m	22,61 m	22,61 m	22,61 m	22,61 m	22,61 m
Length overall	17,38 m	17,50 m	17,51 m	17,51 m	17,51 m	17,51 m
Height	4,10 m	4,10 m	4,20 m	4,20 m	4,20 m	4,20 m
Wing area		87,60 m^2	86,50 m^2	86,50 m2	86,50 m2	86,50 m^2
Weights: Empty	5782 kg	5400 kg	5800 kg	5800 kg	5800 kg	6000 kg
Normal take-off	7590 kg	8209 kg	8600 kg	8600 kg	8600 kg	8800 kg
Engine: Type	2 x BMW VI 6,0 Z	2 x BMW VI 6,0 Z	2 x DB 600 C	2 x DB 600 A	2 x DB 600 CG	2 x DB 600 Ga
Take-off rating [kW (hp)]	2 x 486 (660)	2 x 486 (660)	2 x 699 (950)	2 x 699 (950)	2 x 699 (950)	2 x 773 (1050)
Performance: Max speed/at height [km/h/m]	349/5400	309/5400	370/4000	390/4000	370/4000	410/4000
Cruise speed [km/h]	x	270	340	365	369	370
Landing speed [km/h]	x	110	115	120	115	120
Service ceiling [m]	6000	6000	7000	7000	7000	7000
Max range [km]	1500	2500	1065	1065	1065	1065
Defensive armament	-	3 x 7,9 mm	3 x 7,9 mm	3 x 7,9 mm	3 x 7,9 mm	3 x 7,9 mm
Bomb load	-	1000 kg	1500 kg	1500 kg	1500 kg	1500 kg

Type	He 111 E–3	He 111 F–4	He 111 J–1	He 111 P–2	He 111 P–4	He 111 P–6
Dimensions: Span	22,61 m	22,50 m	22,50 m	22,50 m	22,50 m	22,50 m
Length overall	17,51 m	17,51 m	17,51 m	16,40 m	16,40 m	16,40 m
Height	4,20 m	4,20 m	4,20 m	4,00 m	4,00 m	4,00 m
Wing area	86,50 m^2	86,50 m2	86,50 m2	86,50 m^2	86,50 m^2	86,50 m^2
Weights: Empty	6140 kg	6200 kg	6120 kg	6250 kg	6780 kg	6350 kg
Normal take-off	10500 kg	10600 kg	10550 kg	12700 kg	13500 kg	13000 kg
Engine: Type	2 x Jumo 211 A–1	2 x Jumo 211 A–3	2 x DB 600 Ga	2 x DB 601 A–1	2 x DB 601 Aa	2 x DB 601 N
Take-off rating [kW (hp)]	2 x 791 (1075)	2 x 810 (1100)	2 x 773 (1050)	2 x 810 (1100)	2 x 865 (1175)	2 x 865 (1175)
Performance: Max speed/at height [km/h/m]	420/5000	430/5000[a]	415/5000	410/5000	398/5000	420/5000
Cruise speed [km/h]	380	385	370	380	370	385
Landing speed [km/h]	120	120	120	120	120	120
Service ceiling [m]	8000	8000	7000	8000	8000	8000
Max range [km]	1065	1820	1820	1970	2450	1970
Defensive armament	3 x 7,9 mm	3 x 7,9 mm	3 x 7,9 mm	3 x 7,9 mm	6 x 7,9 mm, 1 x 20 mm	5 x 7,9 mm, 1 x 20 mm
Bomb load	2000kg	2000kg	2000 kg	2000kg	2000kg	2000kg

Type	He 111 H–1	He 111 H–3	He 111 H–4	He 111 H–5	He 111 H–6
Dimensions: Span	22,50 m	22,50 m	22,50 m	22,50 m	22,50 m
Length overall	16,40 m	16,40 m	16,40 m	16,40 m	16,40 m
Height	4,00 m	4,00 m	4,00 m	4,00 m	4,00 m
Wing area	86,50 m^2	86,50 m^2	86,50 m2	86,50 m^2	87,60 m2
Weights: Empty	6300 kg	6700 kg	6850 kg	6950 kg	6800 kg
Normal take-off	12600 kg	13120 kg	14220 kg	15700 kg	13200 kg
Engine: Type	2 x Jumo 211 A–1	2 x Jumo 211 D–1/F–1	2 x Jumo 211 D–1/F–1	2 x Jumo 211 F–1	2 x Jumo 211 F–1
Take-off rating [kW (hp)]	2 x 791 (1075)	2 x 883 (1200)/957 (1300)	2 x 883 (1200)/957 (1300)	2 x 957 (1300)	2 x 957 (1300)
Performance: Max speed/at height [km/h/m]	410/6000	425/435/6000	415/425/6000	405/6000	430/6000
Cruise speed [km/h]	370	375	325-330	330	390
Landing speed [km/h]	125	125	125	125	135
Service ceiling [m]	8000	8000	8500	8500	8500
Max range [km]	2060	2060	2600	3100	2060
Defensive armament	3 x 7,9 mm	7 x 7,9 mm	6 x 7,9 mm	6 x 7,9 mm	6 x 7,9 mm, 1 x 20 mm
Bomb load	2000kg	2000kg	1500kg	500kg	2000 kg[b]

Type	He 111 H–16	He 111 H–21	He 111 H–23	He 111 R–2	He 111 Z–1
Dimensions: Span	22,50 m	22,50 m	22,50 m	22,50 m	35,40 m
Length overall	16,40 m	16,40 m	16,40 m	16,40 m	16,40 m
Height	4,00 m	4,00 m	4,00 m	4,00 m	4,00 m
Wing area	86,50 m^2	86,50 m^2	86,50 m^2	86,50 m^2	147,44 m^2
Weights: Empty	6900 kg	7050 kg	6800 kg	6800 kg	21300 kg
Normal take-off	14000 kg	14000 kg	13200 kg	13000 kg	29700 kg
Engine: Type	2 x Jumo 211 F–2	2 x Jumo 213 E–1	2 x Jumo 213 A–1	2 x DB 603 U	5 x Jumo 211 F–2
Take-off rating [kW (hp)]	2 x 986 (1340)	2 x 1288 (1750)	2 x 1306 (1775)	2 x 1259 (1710)	5 x 986 (1340)
Performance: Max speed/at height [km/h/m]	434/6000	480/7000	490/7000	500/9000	437/6000
Cruise speed [km/h]	390	410	410	470	394
Landing speed [km/h]	135	140	140	140	135
Service ceiling [m]	8500	10000	10000	13000	10200
Max range [km]	2060	2060	2060	1800	4000
Defensive armament	5x7,9mm ,1x13mm, 1x20mm,	4x7,9mm, 3x13mm, 1x20mm	4 x 7,9 mm, 2x13 mm,	6 x 7,9 mm, 1 x 20 mm	6x7,9, 1x13mm, 1x20mm
Bomb load	2000kg[b]	3000kg	1000kg of load	2000 kg	4 – 6 tonnes of load

Uwagi:
In sources specifications, especially performance, are differed.
[a] - without external pylons;
[b] - with overload and range shortage to 650 km or with R–Geräte use raising to 3000 kg.